The York Realist

by Peter Gill

World Première Production

by English Touring Theatre

November 2001

SUPPORTED BY THE NATIONAL LOTTERY THROUGH THE ARTS COUNCIL OF ENGLAND

Funded by THE ARTS COUNCIL OF ENGLAND

English Touring Theatre

English Touring Theatre was set up eight years ago with the aim of bringing quality theatre to as many people as possible throughout the country.

In the past eight years we have toured over twenty productions, and gained a reputation for work which is carefully conceived, true to the play and respects its audience. We have won ten major awards, taken ten productions into London, and worked with some of the most talented and respected artists in the country.

Most of our work has been classical revivals. Our successes include Alan Cumming's *Hamlet,* Kelly Hunter in *As You Like It,* our award winning production of *Hedda Gabler* with Alexandra Gilbreath, both parts of Shakespeare's *Henry IV,* Timothy West and Emma Cunniffe in *The Master Builder,* and Prunella Scales and Michael Feast in *The Cherry Orchard.* We also enjoyed considerable success with the world premières of Jonathan Harvey's *Rupert Street Lonely Hearts Club* and *Hushabye Mountain,* which were seen at the Donmar Warehouse and Hampstead Theatre Club.

At the heart of everything we do is the passionately held belief that quality theatre does not have to be elitist, and that people everywhere expect and deserve the best. This is why in addition to the work on stage we also provide a first class Education Programme to accompany our tours. We are committed to making our work as accessible as possible, and have launched the Friends of English Touring Theatre to celebrate the support we receive from our audience.

We have recently been given a superb new base in London, which we believe will help us do what we are funded for: touring high quality theatre throughout Britain.

Stephen Unwin
Artistic Director

Cast Biographies

Lloyd Owen
GEORGE

Theatre: *Edward II* at the Crucible, Sheffield; *Julius Caesar* at the Young Vic; *The Way of the World* at the Royal Exchange, Manchester; *Morphic Resonance* and *Our Boys* at the Donmar Warehouse; *Closer* at the Lyric, Shaftesbury Avenue; *Who's Afraid of Virginia Woolf?* at the Almeida and the Aldwych; *East Lynne* at Greenwich; *Grab the Dog* at the RNT Studio; *Henry VI part III* for the RSC; Lyubimov's *Hamlet* at the Haymarket and the Old Vic; *Twelfth Night, Macbeth, The Tempest* and *Philoctetes* for Cheek by Jowl

Television: *Hearts and Bones, Gypsy Girl, Get Real, The Cinder Path, All in the Game, The Young Indiana Jones Chronicles, The Story of Frankenstein, Stay Lucky, The Chief, Forever Green, Boon*

Film: *Between Dreams, From the Balcony*

Radio: *'Tis Pity She's a Whore*

Richard Coyle
JOHN

Theatre: *Marat/Sade* at the Theatre Royal, Bristol; *A View from the Bridge* at the Leicester Haymarket; *The Sitcom Festival* at the Riverside Studios

Television: *Macbeth, Hetty Wainthropp Investigates, The Life and Crimes of William Palmer, Greenstones, Wives and Daughters, Up, Rising, Dalziel and Pascoe, Hearts and Bones, Coupling, Sword of Honour, Lorna Doone, Othello*

Radio: *A Lovely Evening, A Look Across The Eyes*

Film: *Jane Eyre, What Rats Won't Do, Human Traffic, Topsy-Turvy, Young Blades, Happy Now?*

Anne Reid
MOTHER

Theatre: *A Family Affair* at the Theatre Royal, Bath and tour; *Blithe Spirit* at the Palace, Watford; *Wild Oats* at the RNT; *Enjoy* at the Nottingham Playhouse; *A Passionate Woman* at the West Yorkshire Playhouse; *Noises Off* at Birmingham Rep; *A Taste of Honey* and *Billy Liar* at the Bolton Octagon; *Pride and Prejudice* at the Theatre Royal York and tour

Television includes: *Linda Green, Sweet Charity, Hearts and Bones, Dinnerladies, Victoria Wood - And All the Trimmings, Dalziel and Pascoe, Peak Practice, Lost for Words, Spark, Playing the Field, Heartbeat, Pat and Margaret, Paul Merton in..., Hetty Wainthropp Investigates, Roughnecks, Ruth Rendell Mysteries, Victoria Wood As Seen on TV* and *Comedy Playhouse, The Wingless Bird, Sometimes Never, Rich Tea and Sympathy, A Bit of Fry and Laurie, Firm Friends, Inappropriate Behaviour, Dr Who, The Bill, Bleak House, Coronation Street*

Film: *Liam, Love and Death on Long Island, The Infiltrator, A Close Shave*

Caroline O'Neill
BARBARA

Theatre: *Vertigo* at the Theatre Royal; *One More Wasted Year* and *Stranger's House* at the Royal Court; *The Ladies of the Corridor* at the Finborough Arms; *Moses, Napoleon and the Queen* and *Increased Difficulty*

The York Realist

'If it hadn't been for the York realist, Shakespeare would have been a third rate playwright like Goethe'.

I remember Peter Gill cracking this joke fifteen years ago. He had invited me to direct Goethe's extraordinarily intellectual *Torquato Tasso* at the National Theatre Studio, and I could tell that the provocation was intended as part of my ongoing education. But like all the best lessons it took me a while to work out what it meant. However, as soon as I heard that Peter had written a play called *The York Realist,* I knew that I wanted to read it, and that English Touring Theatre should do it.

Peter Gill is part of that astonishing group of actors, directors and writers who converged on the Royal Court in London in the 1950s and 1960s and made it one of the great theatres of the world. This was the theatre that produced John Osborne's *Look Back In Anger,* Arnold Wesker's *Roots,* Edward Bond's *Saved,* the plays of David Storey and Peter Gill's productions of the world premières of the DH Lawrence Trilogy: *The Daughter-in-Law, The Widowing of Mrs Holroyd* and *A Collier's Friday Night.*

One of the striking features of the Royal Court in the 1960s was that many of the people involved came from working class backgrounds. Regional accents were not simply accepted, they were celebrated. The Royal Court's commitment to realism meant that no kind of experience was to be excluded, which is not to say that it was naïve - the Royal Court was an 'art theatre', which changed the entire aesthetic of the British theatre. But this was a theatre committed to giving a voice to a part of society that had not been heard, and it astonished its audiences by the passionate rawness of its work on stage.

Of course, the Royal Court never claimed that this was new, it just felt new after the theatre of the 1940s and 1950s. In fact, it connected to a very old alternative tradition in English drama, which culminated in those extraordinary scenes in Shakespeare in which working men and women, in their own dialect, speak their hearts and souls. Its deepest roots lie in the English medieval drama, especially the great Mystery Cycles of Coventry, Wakefield and York. It is not known who wrote the Mystery plays, which were staged by the Medieval guilds, but you can detect in the York Cycle a writer of extraordinary talent, whose work is characterised by a tough, realistic style: the soldiers nailing Christ on the cross speak in a flinty vernacular and the shepherds watching their flocks are shepherds on a Yorkshire moor. The work of the 'York realist' transforms these Catholic, spiritual dramas into secular celebrations of community.

Peter Gill's play *The York Realist* is set in York in the early 1960s. At its heart is a love story between the middle class Londoner John - who has come to York to work as Assistant Director on an amateur staging of the York Mystery plays - and the working class George, who is acting in it. John wants George to leave York and move down to London with him, where he is working in the theatre, quite possibly the Royal Court. In George's decision, Peter Gill makes us think more deeply about the depth of English class allegiances, the meaning of family, the complex relationship between London and the 'regions', and the origins and ownership of art itself.

Stephen Unwin

Cast, Creative & Production Team

Lloyd Owen	GEORGE
Richard Coyle	JOHN
Anne Reid	GEORGE and BARBARA'S MOTHER
Caroline O'Neill	BARBARA
Ian Mercer	ARTHUR
Wendy Nottingham	DOREEN
Felix Bell	JACK

Peter Gill	DIRECTOR
William Dudley	DESIGNER
Hartley T A Kemp	LIGHTING DESIGNER
Terry Davies	COMPOSER
Josie Rourke	ASSISTANT DIRECTOR
Jeanette Nelson	DIALECT COACH
Toby Whale	CASTING DIRECTOR

The YORK REALIST is set in a farm labourer's cottage outside York in the early 1960s.

THE YORK REALIST received its world première on 15 November 2001 at The Lowry, Salford Quays.

Simon Curtis	PRODUCTION MANAGER
Rupert Barth Von Wehrenalp	TECHNICAL MANAGER
Annabel Ingram	COMPANY STAGE MANAGER
Claire Casburn	DEPUTY STAGE MANAGER
Maxine Foo	ASSISTANT STAGE MANAGER
Jai Lusser	TECHNICAL STAGE MANAGER
Margie Bailey	WARDROBE SUPERVISOR
Joan Hughes	WARDROBE MISTRESS
Malcolm Rippeth	PRODUCTION ELECTRICIAN
Sara Perks	PROPS AND SET DRESSING
Stagesign	BSL INTERPRETATION
Vocaleyes	AUDIO DESCRIPTION
Ivan Kyncl	PRODUCTION PHOTOGRAPHY
Erika van Doorn	STAGE MANAGEMENT WORK PLACEMENT from Bristol Old Vic Theatre School

Awards

In its first eight years English Touring Theatre has won ten major awards and received numerous nominations:

BARCLAYS/TMA THEATRE AWARDS
BEST ACTOR Alan Cumming *Hamlet*
BEST ACTRESS Kelly Hunter *As You Like It*
BEST TOURING PRODUCTION *Hedda Gabler*
BEST ACTRESS IN A SUPPORTING ROLE Emma Cunniffe *The Master Builder*

SUNDAY TIMES IAN CHARLESON AWARDS
FIRST PRIZE Alexandra Gilbreath *Hedda Gabler*
FIRST PRIZE Mark Bazeley *The Seagull*

MANCHESTER EVENING NEWS AWARDS
BEST ACTOR Bette Bourne *The Importance of Being Earnest*
BEST NEW PLAY *Rupert Street Lonely Hearts Club*
BEST ACTOR IN A TOURING PRODUCTION Timothy West *The Master Builder*

CITY LIFE AWARD
BEST PLAY *Rupert Street Lonely Hearts Club*

Andrew Lincoln in *Hushabye Mountain*

of Concentration at the Old Red Lion; *Watch Out for Mr Stork* at Regent's Park; *The Lion, the Witch and the Wardrobe* at the Mermaid; *And His Name was Jim* at the Grove

Television: *Waking the Dead, Peak Practice, Coronation Street, Blood Strangers, Doctors, Holby City, Hollyoaks, Where the Heart Is, Queer as Folk, Wing and a Prayer, Birds of a Feather, Cops, Maisie Raine, The Bill, Out of Line, Shine on Harvey Moon, Landmarks, The Bill, Here Comes the Mirror Man, The Detectives, Body and Soul, Heartbeat, Dead Romantics, The Secret, Coasting, Grange Hill, Assert Yourself*

Ian Mercer
ARTHUR

Theatre: *Romeo and Juliet* at the Young Vic; *The Revenger's Tragedy, The Rivals* and *Chips With Everything* at the West Yorkshire Playhouse; *Saturday Night, Sunday Morning* at Nottingham Playhouse; *Spend, Spend, Spend* at the Oldham Coliseum; *The Fancy Man* at Hampstead Theatre Club; *Welcome Home* for Paines Plough; *Rat in the Skull* at the Crucible, Sheffield; *Billy Liar* and *Stop the Children's Laughter* at the Bolton Octagon

Television: *Shackleton, Coronation Street, A Touch of Frost, Cracker, Common as Muck, Brick is Beautiful, Night Voice, The Monocled Mutineer, Flowers in the Rain, Oi for England, Starting Out, Floodtide, Blue Honey*

Film: *Rough Auntie, Shooting Stars, Alex and the First Day*

Wendy Nottingham
DOREEN

For English Touring Theatre: *Rupert Street Lonely Hearts Club* at the Criterion

Theatre: *The Madness of Esme and Shaz* and *Ambulance* at the Royal Court; *It's a Great Big Shame* at Stratford East; *The Way of the World* at the Lyric, Hammersmith; *The Shaughraun* and *The Voysey Inheritance* at the RNT; *Jane Eyre* at the West Yorkshire Playhouse; *The Crucible* at the Young Vic Studio

Television: *Casualty, Kiss Me Kate, Extremely Dangerous, People Like Us, The Peter Principle, McCallum, A Wing and a Prayer, The Bill, The Pale Horse, The Sculptress, Bliss, The Vet, Bramwell, The Wimbledon Poisoner, Kinsey, Shrinks, A Very Peculiar Practice, What's Got Into You, Tumbledown, Precious Bane, Short and Curlies*

Film: *Topsy-Turvy, Secrets and Lies, Mary Reilly*

Felix Bell
JACK

Theatre: *The Secret Garden*

Television: *Holby City, Cold Feet, The People's Harry Enfield, Cry Wolf, All Along the Watchtower, Unfinished Business, Dangerfield, Mothertime, It Happened Next Year, LRTV, Prime Suspect, Rory Bremner Who Else?, The Fast Show, Mother's Day*

Film: *Potemkin, The Secret Garden*

Radio: *The Bunker, Wuthering Heights*

Creative Team Biographies

Peter Gill
PLAYWRIGHT/ DIRECTOR

Theatre includes: For the RNT: *Luther, A Month in the Country, Don Juan, Much Ado About Nothing, Danton's Death, Major Barbara, Tales from Hollywood, Small Change, Kick For Touch, Antigone, Venice Preserv'd, Fool for Love, The Murderers, As I Lay Dying, A Twist of Lemon, In the Blue, Bouncing, Up for None, The Garden of England, Show Songs, Mean Tears, Mrs Klein, Juno and the Paycock, Cardiff East* and *Scrape Off The Black;* For the Royal Court: *A Collier's Friday Night, The Local Stigmatic, The Ruffian on the Stair, A Provincial Life, A Soldier's Fortune, The Daughter-in-Law, The Widowing of Mrs Holroyd, Life Price, The Sleeper's Den, Over Garden's Out, The Duchess of Malfi, Crete* and *Sergeant Pepper, The Merry-Go-Round, The Fool* and *Small Change;* For the Riverside Studios: *The Cherry Orchard, The Changeling, Measure for Measure, Julius Caesar;* For the RSC: *Twelfth Night, New England* and *A Patriot for Me;* At the Queen Elizabeth Hall: *Bow Down* and *Down by the Greenwood Side;* For Opera North: *The Marriage of Figaro;* For the Lyric, Hammersmith: *The Way of the World;* For Field Day: *Uncle Vanya;* For the Almeida: *Tongue of a Bird* and *Certain Young Men;* For the New Ambassadors: *Speed-the-Plow*

Plays include: *The Sleeper's Den, Over Gardens Out, Small Change, Kick For Touch, In The Blue, Mean Tears, Cardiff East, Certain Young Men, Friendly Fire, The Look Across The Eyes, Lovely Evening*

Adaptations and Versions: *A Provincial Life, The Merry-Go-Round, The Cherry Orchard, Touch And Go, As I Lay Dying, The Seagull*

Terry Davies
COMPOSER

For English Touring Theatre: *Hushabye Mountain, The School for Scandal*

Theatre: For the RSC: *Alice in Wonderland, A Patriot for Me, New England* and *Coriolanus;* For the RNT: *Luther, The Rise and Fall of Little Voice, The Misanthrope, Neaptide, The Festival of New Plays, Antigone* and *Tales from Hollywood;* For Regent's Park: *Love's Labour's Lost, Much Ado About Nothing, A Midsummer Night's Dream* and *Twelfth Night; The Lady in the Van* at the Birmingham Rep; *Speed-the-Plow* at the Duke of York's; *Alarms and Excursions* at the Gielgud; *Tongue of a Bird* at the Almeida; *Kes! - The Musical* for Bolton Octagon and York Theatre Royal; *The Snow Queen* at Theatr Clywd; *Goldhawk Road* at the Bush; *Uncle Vanya* for Field Day; *The Way of the World* at the Lyric, Hammersmith; *Richard III* for the Icelandic National; *The Birds - A Musical* for Istanbul City Theatre

Dance: *The Car Man*

Film: As Orchestrator / Conductor: *The Magic of Vincent, The Lawless Heart, The Parole Officer, The Sleeping Dictionary, Born Romantic, A Midsummer Night's Dream, The War Zone, Perdita Durango, Cousin Bette* and *Photographing Fairies*

William Dudley
DESIGNER

Theatre includes: For the Royal Court: *Small Change, The Fool, Edmund, Hamlet, Etta Jenks, Kafka's Dick, I Licked A Slag's Deodorant;* For the RSC: *Ivanov, That Good Between Us, Richard III, The Party, The Merry Wives Of Windsor, Richard II, A Midsummer Night's Dream, Country Dancing, The General From America, Marya, Hamlet, The Ship* and *The Big Picnic;* In the West End: *I Claudius, Mutiny!, Kiss Me Kate, Girlfriends, Matador, Heartbreak House, My Night With Reg,*

Rat In The Skull, A Streetcar Named Desire, Lenny, Entertaining Mr Sloane and *Blue/Orange;* For the RNT: *Lavender Blue, Larkrise To Candleford, Lost Worlds, The World Turned Upside Down, Undiscovered Country, Dispatches, Don Quixote, Schweyk In The Second World War, The Real Inspector Hound, The Critic And The Mysteries, Entertaining Strangers, Waiting For Godot, Cat On A Hot Tin Roof, The Shaughraun, The Changeling, Bartholomew Fair, The Voysey Inheritance, The Crucible, The Coup, Pygmalion, The Rise And Fall Of Little Voice, On The Ledge, Johnny On A Spot, Under Milk Wood, Wild Oats, Mary Stuart, The Alchemist, The Homecoming, The London Cuckolds, Cleo Camping Emmanuelle And Dick, The Forest, Blue/Orange* and *All My Sons; Some Sunny Day* at Hampstead; *The Deep Blue Sea* and *Tongue Of A Bird* at the Almeida; *Amadeus* at the Old Vic and Broadway; *The Dance Of The Vampires* in Vienna

Opera includes: *Idomeneo* for WNO; *Billy Budd* for Metropolitan Opera; *Barber Of Seville* and Seraglio at Glyndebourne; *Tales Of Hoffman, Der Rosenkavalier, Don Giovanni* and *The Cunning Little Vixen* at the ROH; *The Ring Cycle* at Bayreuth; *Un Ballo In Maschera* at the Salzburg Festival; *Lucia Di Lammermoor* in Chicago and at Opera National de Paris, *The Silver Tassle* for the ENO

Film: *Persuasion, The Rose Theatre*

Hartley T A Kemp
LIGHTING DESIGNER

Theatre: For the Almeida: *Certain Young Men, Tongue of a Bird* and *The Doctor's Dilemma;* For the RSC: *The Merchant of Venice;* For the Donmar Warehouse: *Passion Play* and *Good;* For the Crucible, Sheffield: *Don Juan, The Country Wife, As You Like It, A View From the Bridge, Twelfth Night* and *Queuing for Everest;* For the Oxford Stage Company at the Whitehall: *Fifty Revolutions;* For the West Yorkshire Playhouse: *Dealer's Choice;* For the Royal Court Upstairs: *Faith;* for Pluto Productions at the New End: *The Disputation* and *The Queen of Spades and I;* For the Southwark Playhouse: *Thieves Like Us, In the Jungle of Cities, Rosmersholm* and *Seascape with Sharks and Dancer;* At the Tiroler Landestheater, Innsbruck: *Showboat* and *West Side Story;* At the Arts Centre: *Dorian;* At the Theatre Royal, Hanley: *Jesus Christ - Superstar;* At the Old Fire Station, Oxford: *Assassins* and *Sweet Lorraine;* At the Georgian Theatre, Richmond and on tour: *The Happy Prince*

Opera: For the ROH Linbury Studio: *Mary Seacole, Oreste* and *Oresteia;* For Opera Holland Park: *Iris;* For Castleward Opera: *Madame Butterfly, Martha, The Barber of Seville, La Sonnambula* and *Carmen;* For London City Opera, Chichester Festival and on tour: *Die Fledermaus;* For the QEH and on tour: *The Marriage of Figaro*

Hartley is also Artistic Director for C venues at the Edinburgh Festival

Josie Rourke
ASSISTANT DIRECTOR

Theatre as Assistant Director: *Dangerous Corner* at Watford Palace; *Passion Play* at the Donmar Warehouse and the Comedy; *Merrily We Roll Along, Orpheus Descending, To the Green Fields Beyond* and *Boston Marriage* at the Donmar Warehouse

Theatre as Director: *Johan Padan and the Discovery of the Americas* at the Dario Fo Festival; *Henry IV Part I* at the Edinburgh Festival; *The Wrong Side of the Rainbow* at the Donmar Warehouse

Forthcoming projects as a Director: *Kick for Touch* by Peter Gill for Sheffield Theatres

Theatre for Everyone

An Open Door

English Touring Theatre believes quality productions of great drama should be open to all. At the heart of everything we do is our commitment to national touring.

- We believe there should be no contradiction between artistic integrity and public accessibility, and we aim to produce work which is clear and true to the play.
- Although we have no direct control over ticket prices we try to encourage the venues to address this issue as creatively as possible.
- Our education initiatives have earned a national reputation for creative and innovative work involving thousands of young people each year.
- We run a nationwide programme of special events and training courses hosted by established arts professionals.
- We regularly organise pre-show talks, post-show discussions and workshops which allow members of our audience to gain a deeper insight into the artistic process.
- We provide masterclasses and practical sessions for adults, examining all aspects of language, dramaturgy, historical context and professional theatre practice.
- We offer arts based management training programmes to assist businesses with communication, presentation and interpersonal skills.

Access For All

English Touring Theatre regularly offers events and performances specially designed for visually and hearing impaired audience members. In collaboration with organisations such as Stagesign, SPIT, Minds Eye and Vocaleyes we provide:

- BSL Interpreted and Audio Described performances and events led by qualified professionals.
- Touch Tours providing an Audio Described introduction to characters, set, costumes and props, followed by a guided tour of the stage where participants are able to touch and feel the materials used to create the world of the play.

Friends of ETT

The Friends of English Touring Theatre scheme allows our audience to get more involved with the Company.

The support of our Friends is essential to ETT's continued success. We actively encourage our audience to get involved, and we want to give our Friends as many additional benefits as possible. In return we hope our Friends will continue to support us in our aim of touring high quality theatre throughout the country. Every penny you can give will go on stage. Please support us as generously as you can.

Relaunching the Friends scheme earlier this year has proved highly successful, and we are delighted to number Sheila Hancock, Sam Mendes, Trevor Nunn, Prunella Scales, Emma Thompson, Timothy West and Penelope Wilton amongst our Good and Best Friends. However, as we are now producing four shows a year your support and involvement will be more crucial than ever before.

As a Friend of ETT you will receive regular information about our productions and events and a newsletter containing exclusive articles and information.

£50 GOOD FRIEND
For £50 per year, you will receive the benefits enjoyed by Friends, plus:

- Discounts on a wide range of merchandise including books and educational resource materials
- Loyalty discounts - the more years you are a Good Friend the larger the loyalty discounts you will receive
- Exclusive "Friend Only" ticket discounts at your local theatre for all ETT productions
- Automatic entry into regular prize draws and competitions

£100 BEST FRIEND
For £100 per year, you will receive the benefits enjoyed by Friends and Good Friends, plus:

- Invitations to "meet the cast and creative team" evenings at a tour venue near to you
- Free programmes and posters mailed direct to your door in advance of the performance
- Your name listed in our programmes
- Invitations to ETT's Christmas Party and other exclusive events

ETT's London Base

In July of this year English Touring Theatre moved its offices to London.

The Company enjoyed a long and fruitful residency in Crewe, Cheshire, for eight years, but the opportunity provided by the National Lottery (through the Arts Council of England) of a superb, rent-free, purpose built base right in the heart of Waterloo was too good to miss. We are confident that it will help consolidate our position as the leading touring theatre company in Britain.

Some people have thought that this move will mean that the company will stop touring, or perform exclusively in London. In fact the opposite is the case. We are as committed as ever to touring high quality productions. Furthermore, we have recently been awarded an increase in our Arts Council funding which will allow us to tour four productions a year and increase the number of education initiatives nationwide.

In addition to excellent office accommodation, Short Street has a first class rehearsal room and a meeting room, both of which are available to hire.

If you would like more information about these facilities, please contact us at:
English Touring Theatre, 25 Short St, London SE1 8LJ
Phone 020 7450 1990 Fax 020 7450 1991 email admin@englishtouringtheatre.co.uk

Rehearsal room at Short Street during rehearsals for *The Caretaker*

25 Short Street

English Touring Theatre

Patron
Sir Ian McKellen

Board of Directors
Josephine Burns
Keith Burton - *Secretary*
Gillian Diamond
Nic Lloyd
Jeremy Newton - *Chair*
Derek Poppleton
Kully Thiarai
Peter Zombory-Moldovan

English Touring Theatre is proud to participate in the John S Cohen Foundation Bursary for training directors in conjunction with the Royal National Theatre Studio.
Previous trainees are: Mick Gordon, Erica Whyman and Arlette George.

Staff
Stephen Unwin
Artistic Director

Tim Highman
Executive Director

Angela Chrimes
Associate Producer

Lin Sarson
Finance Manager

Sarah Firth
Administration and Tour Coordinator

Brec Walker
Education and Access Coordinator

Drew Colverd
Marketing and Development Coordinator

Annie Roberts
Payroll Clerk

English Touring Theatre
25 Short Street
London
SE1 8LJ
Tel 020 7450 1990
Fax 020 7450 1991

email admin@englishtouringtheatre.co.uk
website www.englishtouringtheatre.co.uk

English Touring Theatre is a member of the Theatrical Management Association

English Touring Theatre Limited
Registered in England 2746850
Registered Charity No. 1016895

Peter Gill

THE YORK REALIST

Peter Gill was born in 1939 in Cardiff and started his professional career as an actor. A director as well as a writer, he has directed over eighty productions in the UK, Europe and North America. At the Royal Court Theatre in the sixties, he was responsible for introducing D. H. Lawrence's plays to the theatre. The founding director of Riverside Studios and the Royal National Theatre Studio, Peter Gill lives in London. His plays include *The Sleepers Den* (Royal Court, London, 1965), *Over Gardens Out* (Royal Court, London, 1968), *Small Change* (Royal Court, London, 1976), *Kick for Touch* (Royal National Theatre, London, 1983), *Cardiff East* (Royal National Theatre, London, 1997), *Certain Young Men* (Almeida Theatre, 1999) and *The York Realist* (English Touring Theatre, 2001).

by the same author

PLAYS ONE
(*The Sleepers Den, Over Gardens Out, Small Change, Kick for Touch, Mean Tears, In the Blue*)

CARDIFF EAST
CERTAIN YOUNG MEN
FRIENDLY FIRE
CALL HER AFTER ME
ORIGINAL SIN

adaptations

A PROVINCIAL LIFE (after Chekhov)
THE CHERRY ORCHARD (by Chekhov)
AS I LAY DYING (after the novel by Faulkner)
THE SEAGULL (by Chekhov)

PETER GILL

The York Realist

The Look across the Eyes

Lovely Evening

ff

faber and faber

This collection first published in 2001
by Faber and Faber Limited
3 Queen Square London WC1N 3AU
Published in the United States by Faber and Faber Inc.
an affiliate of Farrar, Straus and Giroux LLC, New York

Typeset by Country Setting, Kingsdown, Kent CT14 8ES
Printed in England by Mackays of Chatham plc, Chatham, Kent

A CIP record for this book is available
from the British Library

0-571-21208-5

2 4 6 8 10 9 7 5 3 1

Contents

THE YORK REALIST

For Bill

Characters

George

John

Mother
to George and Barbara

Barbara

Arthur

Doreen

Jack

The play is set in a farm labourer's cottage outside York in the early 1960s.

One

The living room of a farm labourer's cottage. Leading out of this is a small kitchen which was once the scullery. In the living room, stage right, is an outer door and a window. Left, there is a dresser. At the back is a range no longer used for cooking and, next to this on the left, is a door which opens onto a staircase. To the right is a door into the kitchen where there is a sink under the window, and above the sink a gas water-heater. Nearby, a gas stove and an outer door.

Late afternoon.

George and John in the living-room. George having just let John in.

George Well.

John Yes.

George Aye.

John Yeah . . .

George Well then. Mm . . . Yeah . . . Come in.

John I am in.

George No, come in. Sit down.

John I'm all right.

George I must stink. I haven't changed. I only just come in the door.

John I timed it well.

George You did. You timed it well.
I must stink.

John No. What's the matter with you?

George I was just going to have a wash. I'll just put the kettle on and have a wash. OK?
Had your tea?

John I'm all right. You'd better have your tea, though.
Had your tea?

George No. Not yet.
This is a surprise, though. Isn't it, though?

John Perhaps I should have let you know. You still haven't got a phone.

George No.

John I should have . . .

George No. No. No.

John Just as well. I think that might have . . .

George I'm glad you didn't.
What bus did you get?

John I didn't get a bus.

George What?

John I drove.

George You drove?

John Yes. Why shouldn't I drive?

George You didn't like driving a tractor.
You must have set off early, didn't you? That was a bit of a drive.

John What, six miles?

George No, the drive up. You drive up today?

John No. Yesterday.

George You didn't come over yesterday then?

John No. I didn't get here till late.

George You kept your options open.
What you up for then?

John I'm at the Theatre Royal for the week.

George Oh aye. What's that, a play?

John Yes.
I didn't know whether I should come over or not.

George Why not?

John I dunno. Anyway . . .

George It must be a long drive up in a car. It's five hours on the train.

John Yes. Mind you, the motorway makes it easier. Bit . . . bit . . . daunting.

George I should think so. Well, you're not dependent on the bus tonight are you?

John No.

George You couldn't stay here so easy now. Could you?

John No. No. No.

George You wouldn't have the excuse of the bus with the car.

John *We* wouldn't.

George What?

John Have the excuse.

George No.
Aye, if you stayed here now you could have a proper bath.

John Oh.

George Council grant. Put in a bathroom. Cost me nowt.

John Nowt?

George Nowt.

John That'd have pleased you.

George It did.
They want to take that out. (*indicating the fireplace and range*)

John Going to let them?

George No.

John Why?

George I'm not.
Anyway. I won't be a tick. I still have a wash down here. Used to it.
Yes, they offered to take the range out. I wouldn't let them.

John Oh.

George You said you liked it.

John I do.

George Well then. See.
I better get out of these. You all right a minute?

John Yes. Of course I am.

George Then I'll get the tea after.

John Not for me.
Do you make your own tea then?

George Yes, who else?

John I'm sorry about your mother.

George Yes.

John I wrote.

George Yeah.

John You got it?

George Yeah.

John I thought I shouldn't come.

George Why not?

John Oh.
You managing? You all right?

George Aye. Course I am.
Sure you don't want anything?

John No. But you'd better have something.

George Barbara and Doreen. I have to fend them off.

He goes into the kitchen and begins to wash.
John looks at the fireplace.

John I'm glad you didn't let them take this out.
I said . . .
George.

George's Mother comes on through the door, revealing the stairs.

George What say?

John Nothing.

Mother What am I looking for?

John I said I'm glad you haven't taken out the stove.

Mother Oh yes. Clean pinny. I've got it on. Tt. Tt.

John Can I do anything?

George No.

Mother Do you want a clean shirt, George?

John I'm going to the car.

George What?

Mother Do you want a clean shirt?

John I'm going to get something from the car.

Mother George.

John George.

George What?

John I'm going to get something from the car.

George OK.

John exits.

Mother Do you?

George What?

Mother Do you want an evening shirt?
George.

George What?

Mother Do you want a clean shirt?

George Of course I want a clean shirt.

Mother Do you want one of your decent ones?

George You mean am I going out? I might have to go up later to give him a hand. There's a cow about to calve. So I'm not going out. Right?
Where's the towel?

Mother There's a clean one in here.

George comes into the living room wearing different trousers and without a shirt.

George Give us.

Mother Why are you so late? He's got you doing the work of two men.

George There's Charlie. We manage.

Mother He used to have more than you and Charlie. He needs more than two men. He's always been tight. His father was the same.
What shirt do you want?

George It doesn't matter which one I want. I'm not going out.

Mother Aren't you going to your play?
This'll do you, then.

He takes the shirt she offers and puts it on.

Have you shaved?

George Aye. All right? (*Proffers his chin.*)

Mother Yes.

George I need a new packet of blades.

Mother One of them T-shirts do you?

George Nay.

Mother Under your shirt. Arthur wears them.

George Aye, it's a pair of real jeans I'd like. American jeans. Aye, you get them too big, right? You put them on, right? You get in the bath, right? And they shrink to fit you.

Mother See you shrinking jeans in a zinc bath in here. Come on, your dinner's been ready long since.

George My trousers upstairs?

He goes upstairs. She picks up the shirt and towel.

Mother Doreen's supposed to be calling for me later. I don't really want to go.

He comes back down.

George Where's my trousers?

Mother Here's your trousers and your socks.

George What my trousers doing down here?

Mother Come on. Come on.

George Nay, I'm not changing my trousers down here.

Mother I'll save your modesty and get your dinner. I've put it up for you. It's his fault if it's spoiled. I thought you'd be in before this. I swore I heard you whistling.

George You sit down. I'll get it.

Mother No.

George You're supposed to be taking things easy.

Mother I can't be doing nothing all day. I only just made the beds. I had a lie-down.

George Don't give me too much now.

Mother I already put it up. I told you.

Exits to the kitchen. He changes his trousers.

Mother Did you bring me some milk?

George Yes. Yes. Of course I brought you some milk. Do I ever forget?

She enters with his dinner, holding the plate with a tea towel.

Mother That b— door. That oven door out there . . .

George Mother.

Mother Now watch the plate, it's hot.

George Put these on the line, Mother. (*Gives her his trousers and sits down to eat.*)

Mother They need washing.

George No. Just put them on the line.

Mother No. I'll wash them. They're rotten. They wash easy, these.

George You want a washing machine.

Mother What would I do with a washing machine?

George One of them Rolls. I'm getting you one of them.

Mother No.
Mind you, our Barbara, she swears by hers.

George I'm getting you one. They're cracking. They're not a lot. Weekly they're not.

She goes out into the kitchen with the dirty things.

Hey, Mother. They're going on holiday, the gaffer and her.

Mother (*coming back in*) She always goes on holiday.

George Aye. But they're going to Spain, both of them.

Mother What's wrong with Bridlington?
It's nice for some. He won't go. Who's going to manage for him? He's too mean.

George I shan't worry, me.

Mother He won't go. He'd have to get someone in.
What happened to your play? You haven't been going to your play. Isn't it tonight you go?

George No.

Mother You never went last week neither.

George I know. I never went the week before either.

Mother No.

George You were bad.

Mother That was no reason not to go.

George Leave off, Mother.

Mother It's no bother to me. I thought you'd never stick it.

Barbara comes in through the back door and into the living room.

Mother Is that you, Barbara?

Barbara You seen my lad, Mother?

Mother No.

Barbara You had my lad with you, George?

Mother Don't eat so fast, George. Don't be such a guts.
Do you want a cup of tea, Barbara? I'm going to make one now.

Barbara Have you?

George No. He's too old for us now. I haven't seen him for weeks. We could do with him, too.

Barbara He hasn't been to school.

Mother He should go to school.

Barbara Didn't you give him his dinner up here?

Mother No. I haven't seen him.

Barbara He's going wild, he is.

Mother He's not wild. He's not. He's not a bad lad. He's in with some bad uns on that estate. That's what it'll be. I couldn't live down there.

Barbara Well, I wouldn't like to live stuck up here again, I can tell you, Mother, like you, without a bath and a lavatory outside.

Mother Hear that, George?

Barbara I thought he'd had his dinner up here.

Mother He'll not have gone far. You know lads. Anyway, he finishes school soon. He'll soon be working.

Barbara I thought he might start work with you. Arthur don't want it.

Mother It's hard work on a farm.

Barbara Lucky there's plenty of work about.

Mother Put him to a trade. You can't go wrong.
Have you finished?

George Yes. Nothing wrong with that, Mother.

She takes his plate.

Mother Do you want afters?

George Aye. Go on.

Mother Doreen made me a pie.

Barbara Did she? Hear that, George? Doreen's made you a pie.

Mother She's got a touch with pastry.

George And you, Mother. You have.

Mother I had one time. I can't go baking now. (*She goes into the kitchen and brings back a pie. She serves George a slice.*)

Barbara Doreen making you pies now then, George.

George You can shut it an' all.

Mother Here we are.

Barbara You want custard with that.

Mother He won't have custard. He don't like custard.

George What do you mean, I don't like custard?

Mother You don't. Do you want custard?

George No.

Mother Do you want Carnation?

George Aye.

Mother See, he don't like custard.

George That doesn't mean I don't like custard.

Mother Where's the Carnation?

George Telling me what I like.

Mother I'm your mother. I know what you like.

Barbara And don't you see he gets it, Mother.

Mother Now. Now. You. (*She goes out to get the Carnation and then goes back to make the tea.*)

Barbara Our George'll never get married, Mother. You spoil him too much.

Mother Aye.

Barbara Will you, George?

George I got it too good here, Barbara.

Barbara You have.

George And I've seen too much of other people's marriages, Barbara. You and Arthur, for one.

Barbara Oh, you can be nasty.
He can be nasty sometimes, Mother.

Mother gives Barbara and George tea.

Mother What lasses are there round here for him, anyway?

Barbara Doreen.

Mother Do you think?

Barbara She made him a pie. I don't know what he's waiting for.

George I'll not leave you, Mother.

Barbara You know when you're on to a good thing.

George Aye.

Mother You've got more sense.

Barbara You'll be fifty before you know it, wearing glasses and thinking you're eighteen.

George She's a cheeky bitch. Keep this shut a bit, Barbara.

Mother Still, I'd like to see him settled. Someone's missing a good husband.
He doesn't go to his play now, Barbara. That journey's too long for him. I said.

Barbara No, it's not. You catch the right bus.

Mother Right into York.

George Hey. Hey. I'm here, you know.

Mother I knew he'd never stick it.

Barbara Doreen put him in for that an' all.

Mother Well, he was good in that play she put on. Very good.

Barbara He was.

Mother All that way into York with his work, I knew he wouldn't make it.

Barbara No. Well, I'd better go, I suppose.

Mother Finish your tea, love.
Doreen's calling for me later. I promised her I'd go to fellowship with her. I don't feel up to it.

Barbara You'll like it when you get there.

George You didn't used to go to chapel so much, Mother.

Barbara Doreen's very keen on chapel.

Mother I've always gone to chapel.

George On a Sunday, aye.

Mother Here, give me your plate. It wouldn't do you any harm to go to chapel either.

Arthur comes in through the back door and into the living room.

Arthur Don't we get any tea?

Mother Hello, Arthur. (*She goes out.*)

Arthur Stay single, George. You get your tea. No question.

Mother Do you want a cup of tea, Arthur?

Barbara I'll be down. I've been looking for our Jack.

Arthur Well, you just missed him.

Barbara What?

Arthur He's been in and out.
The girls want their tea.

Barbara I'll be down now. Wait till I get hold of him. Where did he go?

Arthur I think he said he was going over, you know . . . What's his name? What's he done anyway? What's up?

Barbara He's not going to school. That's what's up.

Arthur I thought he was a bit quick out.
Nice walk up. Hawthorn's thick. Needs someone down that small field, hedging.

George Oh aye. Let him do that.

Arthur Needs doing. Nice up here, this weather.

Barbara Oh, don't start. You were glad to get out. You don't want to live in that old place up there, do you? You don't want to have to work like our George, do you?

Arthur No. No. Nine-to-five. Nine-to-five. Can't beat it, George.

George You're on shift work.

Arthur Yes. Still.

Barbara Well, what we going to do with that little ferret? It won't be long now before he leaves school. What's he going to do then?

Arthur There's plenty of jobs.

Mother He'll be all right. He can go with George, comes to it.

Arthur He'll not go labouring on a farm, I can help it. He can come to work with me.

Barbara See?

Mother Do you want some pie, Arthur?

Arthur Aye.

Barbara We're going now.
It'll spoil your tea.

Mother gives him some pie.

Arthur You going for a pint later, George?

George I don't know, Arthur. He might want me up there.

Mother You two and your drinking.

Barbara They don't drink much, Mother.

Mother What's too much, some might say.

George Oh, Mother, don't go on. That's chapel talking.

Mother Ay. Ay. Arthur's family was all chapel.

Arthur Aye.

Barbara Father didn't go to chapel much, did he?

Mother What do you know about your father?

George Well, he wasn't much of a chapel man, Mother.

Mother What do you know?

George I know.

Mother No, he didn't, more's the pity.

Arthur Ay. I tell you who was a big chapel man. Skepwith. Remember him? When I worked for him?

George Aye.

Arthur He was a right primitive. Always trying to get the men to sign the pledge. Aye. True.

Doreen knocks and comes in through the front door.

Doreen Oooo.

Barbara Hello, Doreen.

Arthur Hello, Doreen, how are you?

Mother I'm not ready, Doreen. What's the time?

Doreen No, I only popped in to see if you'd remembered.

Arthur It's cracking pie, Doreen.

George It is, Doreen.

Barbara Spoil your tea.

Mother No. I haven't forgotten, Doreen.

Arthur Great.

Mother I don't know whether I'm well enough to go, you know, Doreen.

Doreen Oh, I am sorry.

George Go on, Mother. Don't listen to me.

Barbara Aye, go on, Mother. Do you good to go out.

Mother I don't know.

Doreen You'll come with me. She'll come with me. Won't you? We won't be long.

Barbara Come on then, you. If you see our Jack, Mother, if he comes up here, send him home. And you, George. George.

George Aye.

Barbara Hey, Doreen. He's stopped going to his play, you know.

Doreen I didn't know.

Barbara He doesn't go any more, does he, Mother?

Mother No. He doesn't.

Arthur Well, he was good in that play you did, Doreen. He was. How did you get him to do it?

Barbara He was always good at acting in school.

George Hey. I'm here, you know. Why don't you shut up, Barbara?

Doreen Have you stopped going, George?

George I haven't been for a couple of weeks, no.

Mother Too far for him to go.

George No.

Mother Why don't you go then?

George That's my business.

Mother I knew he'd never stick it, Doreen. I don't know how you persuaded him to go in for it in the first place.

Doreen Well, you'll start up again, perhaps.

Arthur Are you coming, then?

Barbara Aye. Tara, then. Tara, Doreen. You spoil him, making him pies.

Doreen Well, I was baking, you know.

Arthur Tara. You going for a pint then, George?

George I don't know. I'll see how it goes up there.

Arthur I might see you, then. I'll be up the Carpenter's.

They exit.

George Right.

Mother You're not going drinking, are you?

George I don't think so. I might. I don't know.
Our Barbara's too nosy.

Doreen Well, I'll call back for you in a minute, shall I?

Mother Aye, go on.

Doreen Won't be long. (*She goes.*)

Mother She's a good girl. But I don't want to go.

George It'll only be an hour.

Mother I've got the pots to do.

George I'll do them, Mother. You go up and get ready.

Mother There aren't many. I'll do them when I get back.

George I'll do them.

Mother Where's my compact?
You should have put a decent shirt on, you going drinking.

George Mother.

Mother Where is it?

She goes out. George clears pots and goes into the kitchen. John knocks on the front door.

George Is that you, Doreen? She's upstairs.

Another knock.

Come in, Doreen.

He goes to the door to find John, who is dressed differently than before.

Oh.

John I'm sorry. I had no other way of getting in touch with you. We only had an address.

George Come in.

John comes into the room.

John Have I come at a bad time? I'm sorry if I've come at a bad time.

George No. No.

John We wondered where you'd been. So I thought I'd come and see you. I just felt I should come and see you.

George How did you get here?

John Bus.

George Not many buses.

John It's no bother. I've come . . . It's just to say you're so good in the play, you see. And we miss you. It's just . . . It's important for everyone to be at rehearsals, you see.

George I know. I should have rung up. I'm sorry about that. No good on the phone.

John No. I'm sure.

Mother enters.

Mother Have you seen my compact, George?
Oh. I thought it was Doreen.

George This is my mother.

Mother There it is. (*She finds the compact.*)

George He's with the play.

Mother Oh. Are you in it too, then?

George No, he's the assistant director.

John Just came to see where George had been.

Mother See, I told you.

George What?

Mother Well, I'll just powder my nose. Excuse me. (*She goes into the kitchen.*)

Doreen comes in.

Doreen Oo. Oo. You ready? Oh.

Mother I won't be a minute, Doreen. Just tidying myself up.

George He's from the play.
(*to John*) Doreen saw the advert.

John Hello.

George He's the assistant director.

Doreen Oh. That's interesting.

Mother comes in.

Mother He's come to sort out our George.

George Mother.

Mother Well, you ready, Doreen? Where's my coat?

Doreen It's warm, mind. (*She puts her coat on.*)

Mother Right. We won't be long.

Doreen I don't expect you'll be here when we get back.

John No. No. I'll have to be going soon.

Doreen I'm looking forward to the play.

John Good. Good.

Mother Tara then.

John Goodbye.

Mother Don't forget them pots, George.

George Aye.

Mother and Doreen exit.

They've gone to chapel. Doreen, she's very chapel-minded. She told me about the play. Do you want anything? Can I get you anything?

John No.

George No? Sure?

John Yes.

George So.

Look, I can't come. I'm sorry. I shouldn't have taken it on. I'm sorry. Work and that. I have to keep an eye on my mother. She's not been too good. Sorry. I feel bad to leave her, like, if she's poorly.

John I see. No. I understand. I thought it was . . . we made you unwelcome. Or the other people . . .

George No. They were nice. Everyone. Very nice, all of them. I like Peter. Very interesting man. Doesn't put himself out much, does he? But when he stirs himself he can put his finger on it, can't he. Won't take no when he puts his mind to it. Gives you something to think about and I like that, me. Smokes a lot, doesn't he? Funny how he holds his cigarette.

John Yes.

George Like this. (*Demonstrates, holding an imaginary cigarette between his thumb and forefinger.*)

'Is it an action?'

Jesus is a nice fellow. Well, they all are. No, it's not that. They're all very . . . well . . . They would be . . .

Doctors and that. I felt a bit awkward at first, until I got in the swing of it. That's not it. No. I just can't come. Like I said.

John It's . . . There aren't many people like you in it.

George Like me?

John You're so right, you see. You make it sound right.

George Do I? No.

John You do.

George I'm sorry you had to come all this way.

John No. That's all right. I'm glad I did.

George Aye?

John It's lovely here, isn't it? This must be old. How old, do you think?

George Oh, I don't know. Old, I suppose.

John Is it yours? Your mother's?

George No. Blimey, no. No, it's a tied cottage. Belongs to the farm.

John So you rent it?

George Only a few shillings. Part of the wages order.

John What's that?

George Means you get other things with the job. Milk, like. If I had a working dog or owt . . .

John I like that. (*Points to the fireplace.*)

George Want to take it out, that.

John No, don't. I'm sorry. It's . . . I like it.

George Not what my mother says.

John You could still cook on it, look.

George Aye. Used to, my mother says. Good fire. In winter it's cold up here.

John I bet.

Well, I'd better be going then, I suppose.

George No, stay a bit.

John Shall I? I'll have to watch for the bus.

George There's plenty of buses. I'll see you get a bus. You'll get a bus.

You like it up here, then?

John Beautiful.

George I'm used to it, me.

I've got to go up the farm directly. I'll take you, if you like. Show you the other cottage on the farm. Arthur – my sister's husband – they lived there. His family. Till he was moved to a council house. It's empty now.

John What about these? (*indicating the pots*) You said you'd do them.

George Oh, aye. No, leave it. Don't worry about them. Do them when we come back.

I'm glad you came.

John And me. I mean . . .

George Yes. Come on. You fit? Go the back way.

Two

A couple of hours later. The same evening. Jack is in the kitchen.
Mother and Doreen come in through the front door.

Mother Come in, Doreen.

Doreen I'll not stay long. See you in.

Mother I must have a cup of tea.

Doreen I'll get it.

Mother No. I'll get it.
Who's that in the kitchen? George?

Jack No. It's me, Nan.

Mother What are you doing out there?
It's our Jack.

Jack Having a biscuit, if that's OK.

Mother He's eating my biscuits.
Put the kettle on, Jack. (*She takes off her hat and coat.*)

Jack It's on.

Mother Tea, Doreen? Take your coat off.

Jack comes in.

Doreen I'll not be long.

Jack It's boiling, the kettle. Do you want me to make you tea, Nan?

Mother No, you can't make a good cup of tea.

Jack Oh. Thanks, Nan.

Mother Have you been home? Your mother's been worried to death about you. What's up with you?

Jack Aye. Course I've been home.

Mother What you doing up here, then?

Jack I came to see you, Nan.

Mother Oh. He's full of nonsense. You are. Your mother give you a good clip, I hope.

Jack She gave me an earful. I come up here. Can I stay the night?

Mother He hasn't been to school, Doreen.

Doreen Oh. Why's that, Jack?

Jack Dunno.

Mother George must have gone out with your father.

Jack No. My father's in.

Mother He must have gone up to work then. There's a cow sick or something. He does too much for him up there. They could do with you, Jack. You stopped going, George says.

Jack Yeah.
Where you been? To chapel, Nan?

Mother Fellowship with Doreen. Do you good to go to chapel once in a while. What do you say, Doreen?

Doreen Jack was in my Sunday school class. Weren't you, Jack?

Jack Aye.

Doreen Aren't you glad you came now?

Mother I am. He takes a good meeting.

Doreen He does.

Mother I'll make the tea. The kettle'll boil dry.

Doreen Let me.

Mother No. No. Look, he's left these. He said he'd do the pots.

Doreen I'll do them.

Mother No. No. I'm making the tea. I've done most of them already.

Doreen Go on. Let me do them.

Mother No. Will you have a cup, Jack?

Jack Aye.

She goes into the kitchen with the unwashed cups.

Doreen Well, Jack. You'll be finishing school.

Jack Yes.

Doreen What are you going to do, then?

Jack Don't know.

Doreen You'll not go on the farm with George, then?

Jack No. I don't know what to do.

Doreen You'll find something.

Jack Join the army, I might.

Doreen Oh, really, Jack? No. Will you? See the world. Will you?

Jack No. I don't know. I might, though.

Mother enters with the tea.

Mother Here we are. (*Pours the tea.*)

Doreen Jack says he's joining the army.

Mother Never.

Jack I might.

Mother Biscuit, Doreen?

Doreen Thank you.
I mustn't be long.

Mother Join the army? No. He'll get a job. He's not afraid of work, that's one thing.

George whistles before he and John come in through the back door.

George Hello. Hello.

Mother Hello. You still here, then?

Doreen Well, this is a surprise. We thought you'd be gone.

John No.

George We been all over. The cow calved.
Hey, Jack.

Mother Cup of tea?

George Aye.

Jack Thank you.

Mother Jack, get a cup. Two cups.

Jack exits.

I thought you said you'd do the pots?

George Didn't I do them?

Mother No, you didn't.

John I'm sorry. I got in the way. I'm sorry.

Jack comes in with the cups.

Jack George don't do the washing-up, do he? Do you? Ha.

Mother He can be handy. He can. So you be quiet.

Jack Women's work, that.

Mother Shut it, you.

Doreen Don't you do any washing-up, Jack?

Mother Course he does.

Jack No, the lasses do that.

George Shut it, big man.

Jack D'you have to do much?

George No. I didn't have to do anything. Charlie was back. But he was lucky. I reckon he should've had Humphries out, to have a look at her.

Mother Too mean.

John I've never seen a calf that young.

Doreen Bonny.

John Yes, very.

Mother Here, do you want biscuits?

John Thank you.

George Aye, Mother, we went to have a look at Arthur's old cottage.

Mother Oo. That's falling down.

George He liked it, didn't you?

Mother Did you?

John Yes. I did. I did.

Mother They had a terrible time up there in winter. One thing you can say about this – (*meaning the range*) You can make a good fire if it gets cold.

George How was your meeting, Mother?

Mother Oh, lovely.

George Who took it?

Mother Fred Broadbent.

George Oh, aye.

Mother What was the reading, Doreen?

Doreen looks in the Bible.

Doreen I marked it.
'There is no remembrance of former things. Neither shall there be any remembrance of things that are to come with those who come after.'

George Oh aye.
What do you take that to mean, Mother?

Mother You shut up, you. I think that was very interesting.

George 'Come unto him all ye that labour.' That's what I like to hear.

Mother Makes no difference. You don't go to chapel to hear anything.

Jack What's this play then in York, George? What are they, mystery plays?

George I don't know. Mystery plays. No, don't laugh. Not murder mysteries. What are they, Doreen?

Doreen Don't ask me. John's the one to ask.

George You tell him. You know.

Doreen Well, they're the stories of the Bible and the New Testament. From the Creation to the Last Judgement. Isn't that right?

John That's right.

Jack They old, then?

Doreen Yes. Very old. The time of York Minster.

Jack Who wrote them?

Doreen I don't know.

John No one knows. Some say the monks.

Mother They Roman Catholic plays?

George No. Are they?

John No. Well . . . Um . . .

Jack They're Bible stories, then.

John Yes. Done as plays.

Jack What's the mystery, then?

John Well, each play was done by a guild of tradesmen. Skilled workers. And I suppose they had secrets. Tricks of the trade. I don't really know.

George Like trade unions, Jack.

John That's what they say. I don't know about that.

Jack Was there a farm labourers' play?

John It was all done in the town.

Jack York?

John Yes, and all over. Coventry and Wakefield.

Jack Wakefield?

George Aye, Wakefield.

Jack Blimey, Wakefield.

George Aye. And they did them from dawn till dusk.

Jack No.

George All over York.

Jack No.

George True.

Doreen So you went to see Arthur's old cottage then, John?

George Yes. He liked it. Didn't you?

John I did.

Jack It's falling down.

George No. The roof's still all right.

Mother Did you see a little byre on the side of that cottage, John? Is it there, George?

George Aye, you can see it.

Mother Well, above that byre, that was a place they kept straw and hay. And you could get into that place above the byre from the bedroom of the cottage. Well, years ago, they used to put the kids in there to sleep above the horse, or a cow if they kept one, in the hay. It was warm, you see.

Jack Get out.

Mother They did. That's true. You ask your father.

John I like it. And this too. I like this.

George He says they're going to sell it. Might. Arthur's old place.

Mother Who's going to buy that stuck up there?

John Who owns it, your boss?

George Ha. Ha. No. He's the tenant. The five farms round here are owned by a man from York.

Mother Never see him. You, Doreen?

Doreen No.

Jack I have.

Doreen Fancies himself a bit of a country man. Hunts and that.

Mother Well, he don't live in the big house.

George No. Empty.

Mother Where does he live?

George Old Rectory.

John This is a nice cottage, too. How old is it, do you think?

Mother Must be old.

George He likes the fireplace. Don't you?

Mother Oh, aye. He don't have to clean it. I'd like to take it out. I'd like a grate like Doreen. A nice modern grate. Mind you, it makes a good fire and the boiler works if you needed it.

John I like it.

Mother No. I'd like a modern house. Like Barbara and Arthur got. But I wouldn't want to live down there.

John I like the dresser.

Mother That's years old. I'd like it all modern.

You know Mrs Dorset. Lives by you, Doreen. They had old china. Lustreware. Staffordshire figures. Beautiful old stuff. Do you know, when her mother died she smashed it all with a hammer. Got rid of it all. Everything. Got rid of the old furniture. Got rid of the brass. Chopped up the dresser. Sick of all the years washing and polishing. I don't blame her.

Doreen Well, the man to tell you all about things round here is the man who took the meeting tonight. Mr Broadbent. You know, those old walls where he pens his sheep on the common in bad weather, they were cottages with roofs put up overnight, he says. If you got a roof up overnight you had rights.

Mother They've always been like they are now, as far as I remember.

Doreen And he says they had no stairs. Just a ladder.

Mother That true?

Doreen Yes, apparently.

Mother Well, I can believe it.

Doreen Oh well, I'll have to be off.

Mother All right, dear. Who's going to see Doreen home?

George Jack will.

Mother How you getting home?

John I don't know.

Jack Can I stay here, Nan?

George No.

Mother Can he?

George No. Not tonight. Anyway, who's going to see Doreen home?

Doreen Oh, I'm all right.

Mother No. You see Doreen home, Jack. And mind you go home after. Doreen, see he gets in after, will you?

Doreen Yes. Jack and I will see each other home. Goodnight. It's very kind of Jack. Very nice.

John I hope you'll come and see the play.

Doreen Oh, I'm looking forward to it. Goodnight, then.

Mother Yes. Goodnight.

Jack Tara then.

Doreen Mind you don't miss your bus.

Jack Goodnight, Nan.

Mother Now think on, Jack.

Jack Tara.

Doreen Pleased to meet you.

Jack and Doreen exit.

Mother She's good to me, that girl. Good as gold. She put him in for your play, you know.

John I know.

Mother Well, I'll just wash these and then I'm off to bed.

George We'll do them.

John Yes.

Mother You said you'd do the others and you went walking.

George Don't go on. We'll do them.

Mother I'll just take them out then and get a glass of water. (*She goes into the kitchen with the cups.*) You'll have to watch your bus. You'll miss it. (*She comes back in.*) I said you'll have to be getting your bus.

George He missed the bus half-hour ago.

Mother He never did.

George Yes. Last one's earlier than we thought.

Mother Are you sure?

George He missed it. He'll have to stay here.

Mother Well, you're on the floor unless you want to share.

George Aye. OK with you?

John Yes. Yes.

Mother Are you sure? You'll have to find him a pair of pyjamas. He won't have any pyjamas.

George I'll find him a pair.

Mother I'll get some clean sheets.

George No. Now you go off to bed. Go on.

John I'm so sorry to be a nuisance.

Mother No, love. George should have known about the bus.

George Have you taken your pills?

Mother I'll take them now. Where's the glass for my teeth? Well. Goodnight. You'll be up early, you know. He has to be up. Gets himself up now. Do you want the clock?

George Aye. Better.

Mother It's a bit fast. He's off before I get up now. Doctor's orders. Rest. Rest. Goodnight.

John Goodnight.

George Goodnight, Mother.

She goes upstairs.

John Have I missed the bus?

George I don't know, have you?

John Have I?

George There's one more. She doesn't know.

John Well.

George Yes.
Your eyes are so bright.

John I'm not often in the country.

George Is that what it is, is it, making you look eager, like?

John Yes. Yes, it is. I don't know the country. I find it strange. You wouldn't.

George No. How strange?

John It's as you expect it and at the same time it isn't. The green, for one thing. The hedges and the fields and seagulls so far inland. And the farm. It's all at odds. So old, some of it. I couldn't take it in. It's so old. The stone. The brick. The walls are so old. I couldn't take it in, and then all that pebbledash on the extension. And the cattle shed with the corrugated roof next to the barn with the old stone and the beams and timbers. And the cow smell in the fresh air. And the floors of the cowshed and the smell in the dairy. Such a clinical, cold smell. And the hay in the barn, right up to the roof. Too sweet.

It puzzled me. Just as you thought it would be and yet not. I don't know.

George What about Arthur's cottage?

John I liked it. I did. I did.

George You can see what I can't see. Why did you throw away the flowers you picked?

John Felt silly.

George No.

John Well, then.

George Aye.

John What? Oh.

George Aye. (*Goes towards John.*)

John No.

George Sh.

John I don't know.

George Don't you want to?

John Yes.

George Yes.

John But staying the night.

George It'll be all right.

John Will it?

George Of course it will. Come on. Let's go to bed, shall we?

John Will you come to rehearsals then?

George What, you blackmailing me?

John If you want me to.

George I might. (*Goes towards him.*)

John No.
I'm nervous. It's all . . . Oh . . .

George What, you afraid a copper's going to come up here and arrest us?

John No. Don't be silly.
Yes. No. All right.
Come on, then.

George Hang on.

John What?

George goes into the kitchen. Comes back with a tin of Vaseline.

John What's that for?

George Vaseline. Be prepared.

John No.

George Yeah.

John Will you come to rehearsals?

George That depends on you. Come on.

John What about the noise?

George You noisy, are you?

John Don't be vulgar.

George Don't worry. She sleeps sound.

John Will you come?

George We'll see.
Come on.

They go upstairs.

Three

A month later. Late evening. Mother, Barbara, Doreen, Jack and Arthur come in through the front door.

Arthur Here we are then, Mother. Doreen. Home.

Doreen Thank you.

Arthur Well, we're back. What a night, aye?

Barbara Are you cold, Mother?

Mother Yes, I am.

Barbara I thought it was me.

Doreen I got cold, warm as the evening was.

Barbara I'm chilled to the bone.

Mother You should have worn a vest, Barbara. I warned you.

Barbara Mother.

Mother I put a winter vest on and I'm cold.

Arthur Shall I put a match to the fire?

Mother Aye. Go on.

He does.

Barbara And it was such a glorious day.

Doreen Just get cold sitting, see, summer evenings.

Arthur Still, what a night.

Doreen Wasn't it marvellous? I still can't get over it.

Mother Put the kettle on, Jack.

Jack It's on.

Arthur We should have something stronger. Warm us up. Celebrate.

Mother Drink. That's all you can think of.

Doreen Did you enjoy it, Jack?

Jack Aye, it was cracking.

Arthur We should have taken the girls.

Jack No.

Barbara No. They'd have never sat still. Not all that time. I'm glad we didn't take them, Arthur.

Mother Nay, they'd never have lasted that long.

Arthur I reckon they'd have liked it.

Mother Sit down, Doreen.

Barbara Where you going, Arthur?

Arthur I'm just going out the back. All right? (*Arthur goes out.*)

Mother He arranged very good seats for us though, didn't he?

Doreen He's the assistant director.

Mother He's a good lad. Put our George through his paces. Took our George in hand. Our George did well, and such a cruel part.

Doreen Cruel, the four of them.

Mother Well, I nearly passed out when I saw him. I didn't know where to put myself.

Doreen Well, I thought it was marvellous. Did you enjoy it, Barbara?

Barbara I did. I thought it was great. He started to clap at the end. I didn't know where to put myself. It said not to clap in the programme. Why was that?

Doreen Sacred work, you see. Like *Messiah*, I suppose.

Barbara Oh, aye.

Arthur enters.

Arthur I wish the girls could have seen it.

Mother Nay. They'd not have lasted, Arthur.

Arthur No. I suppose you're right. It would have been too much for them. Pity.

Jack I'm glad, me.

Arthur I'm glad we've got an inside lav.

Barbara Shut up, Arthur.

Arthur It's cold out there. Freezing.

Barbara Have you been to the Abbey ruins before, Mother?

Mother Oh, years ago. I must have.

Barbara I never have. You, Doreen?

Doreen Oh, aye. Always walk from the museum.

Barbara I never have. Jack?

Jack No.

Barbara You ever been there before, Arthur?

Arthur I must have.

Barbara I haven't.

Arthur Go on.
Do you want tea, all of you? (*Goes into the kitchen.*)

Mother They cut quite a lot of the Old Testament out, Doreen.

Doreen Couldn't get it in one evening, you see.

Mother Abraham and Isaac. That's a sad story. Oh, dear. Oh, dear. Breaks your heart.

Barbara I never knew Noah had a wife.

Doreen No. She was funny, wasn't she?

Jack Like our mam when she gets going.

Barbara Cheek.

Jack Aye, Dad?

Arthur What?

Jack Noah's wife, just like our mam.

Arthur Aye.

Jack Or Nan. Bossy.

Mother Cheeky.

Barbara Aye, you.

Mother Nor Pontius Pilate had a wife.

Doreen She was very common, I thought.

Mother What did you like, Jack?

Jack The Devil.

Barbara Yes, you would.

Doreen Jesus was good.

Mother Yes. God had a good voice, didn't he? Very clear. Well, they were all good. There wasn't a weak part.

Doreen It must be a responsibility, playing Jesus.

Barbara Did you recognise that man, Jack?

Jack No.

Barbara Oh, I did. Off the television. I've seen him in something. I know I have.

Arthur enters with the tea.

Did you recognise him, Arthur?

Arthur It was very good. Very good, all of it.
No, I didn't.

Mother You're right, though. A big responsibility.

Doreen For all of them, when you come to think of it.

Barbara Our George was cruel in the crucifixion, though.

Mother Too cruel.

Arthur Very real. Very real.

Mother Too cruel for me. I could have punched our George doing that to him.

Arthur That was clever how they got him down off the cross. One minute he was up there. The next thing he's facing out the Devil. I never saw him get down. Did you?

Barbara No.

Doreen No. I didn't.

Mother No.

Jack Some trick.

Arthur Some magic trick. We'll have to ask George.

Doreen John'll know. He's the assistant director.

Arthur It was very effective, all of it.

Mother It was very Yorkshire, wasn't it? Not that I mind.

Doreen All very Yorkshire.

Jack Jesus Christ wasn't Yorkshire.

Arthur Yes, he was.

Mother No, but you didn't mind.

Jack I didn't mind.

Mother Thank you, Arthur.

Arthur When will they be back?

Barbara Well, he said not long, didn't he?

Mother Our George is tired. Rehearsals and that. Up early and all that. He must be exhausted.

Barbara You look exhausted, Mother. I don't know about George. You must be ready for bed.

Mother Don't shove me off to bed. I haven't finished my tea.

Barbara You must be careful, Mother.

Mother Careful?

George and John come in.

George Aye. Aye.

John Hello.

Doreen Well done.

Barbara Well done.

Arthur Aye.

Jack Aye.

Mother Very good.

Doreen Very good.

Arthur Aye.

Jack Aye.

George What you got the fire lit for?

John You got cold. I was afraid you would.

Doreen Oh, it was worth it.

John Did you like it?

Doreen Aye, I did.

Mother You were a cruel bugger, George.

George Thanks.

Arthur Hey, George. How did he get down off the cross? That's what's puzzling us.

George You'll have to ask John.

Arthur John?

John I can't. Trade secrets.

Jack There's two men.

John No.

Jack There is. There must be.

Barbara Be quiet, Jack, and come on now, we'll have to go.

Jack Well, what's the assistant director do, like?

Doreen He assists the director.

Jack What does the director do, then?

Barbara Shut up, Jack.

George Well, like what Doreen does in chapel shows.

Barbara You know, you were in that play.

Jack No. But what do you do?

John Not a lot.

George He does. He does.

Mother Chase our George up.

George Aye.

Barbara Come on then.

Doreen I'll come with you. Yes. Well done.

Arthur Yes, well done.

Barbara Well done. We were really proud of you, you know.

Arthur Aye, George, when you going on the stage?

Doreen Aye.

Mother He's been a cruel thing tonight. Bad bugger. I didn't know you could be like that.

George Three other actors, Mother.

Mother Yeah, but I could see you enjoying it. Callous. You did.

George That's training, see. Special rehearsals.

Arthur Aye.

John Why didn't you come back at the end?

Arthur You see? I wanted to.

Barbara Mother and Doreen wouldn't, and I wouldn't.

Arthur I wanted to come back. See backstage.

Jack Aye.

John I kept my eye out for you.

Barbara We couldn't do that, could we?

Mother No.

George Yes. Doreen, you'd have liked it.

John Another time. Come again.

Doreen Oh. I don't know.

Barbara Come on then. Goodnight all. You coming, Doreen?

Doreen Yes.

Arthur Goodnight. Well done.

Barbara Yes.

Doreen Where's my bag?

Barbara Jack?

Jack Aye.

Doreen Goodnight. Thank you.

Barbara Night, Mother.

Mother Night.

Barbara, Doreen, Arthur and Jack go out of the back door.

Mother Oo, I'm tired.

George You looked tired.

Mother Barbara said that, but I wasn't taking any notice of her. She's got too much to say for herself.

George I'll get you a glass of water.

Mother Aye.

George goes into the kitchen.

I did enjoy that, John. Well done.

John Thank you.

Enter George with a glass of water.

Mother Hurry up, love. I feel worn out.

George Here's your glass and your tablets. Do you want a hot-water bottle?

Mother No. Aye.

George Want me to do you one?

Mother Aye.

John I'll do it.

Mother You don't know where it is.

John I do. It's on the hook out there. (*He goes into the kitchen.*)

George You all right?

Mother Aye. Just tired.

George I'll bring it up to you.

Mother Will you? Goodnight, love.

George Goodnight.

Mother Goodnight, John. I'll see you in the morning.

John Yes.

Mother (*to John*) You can have a lie-in. You can.

John comes in.

(*to George*) You'll be tired out, you will.

John Goodnight.

Mother You're not going tomorrow, are you, John?

John No. Wednesday.

George Oh. You're not going Wednesday, are you?

Mother Goodnight. (*She goes upstairs.*)

George Are you, then? Stay, aye? You can stay for a bit, can't you? Holiday. What they say? A break. You've been working hard.

John Not as hard as you.

George Can't you?

John I can't stay, George.
Shall I let the fire go out?

George Aye. Well then.

John What?

George Well, what we going to do?

John About what?

George Oh. Fuck off, John.

John What can we do?

George Stay up here.

John I can't stay up here.

George Don't go. I don't want you to go. You're . . . You . . . Like . . . Mmm . . . Oh, don't.

John Don't. We can't go on now. We're tired. Aren't you tired?

George Good tired, though.
Stay, can't you? You don't have anything to go back for.

John Well, I hope I will have.

George What'll I do? What, aye? Not for ever . . . A bit . . . You see . . . Stay here with me.

John I can't.

George I know. I don't know why I asked.

John Come on. Clear the cups.

John goes into the kitchen. George clears the cups.

George Will you stay till the end, then? Will you?

John Yes. (*He brings in a hot-water bottle.*) Here's the hot-water bottle. Say it's hot.

George takes the hot-water bottle upstairs. John finishes clearing the cups and washes them. George comes down.

I feel as if I live here.
She asleep?

George No. She's worn out, though.

John I wonder, she never says anything. None of them.
It doesn't bother you, does it?

George What? No, it doesn't bother me. You?

John Not with you. But hasn't it ever bothered you? I don't think it has. I don't. Has it?

George No. But I don't look into things like you do.

John Wasn't it hard for you, ever?

George Not really. It wasn't. No. Until I was eighteen I never thought about it. I went out with my mate one night. Next village, after lasses. And we got nowhere and we was full of it. Full of it. It'll have to be you then, I said. And we come home. Home here. Yeah. And it was. And after. It was all right for me. But it wasn't for him. Took it for granted after that.

John Do you see him?

George Aye. And you do.

John Do I what?

George It was Arthur.

John What?

George We were farm boys.
He thinks it never happened. I got on with it.
Is this going to be it when you go?

John Come on, why should it? You can come down to see me. Write to me.

George Aye. I'm a great letter-writer, me.

John Well, George, what can I do?

George Aye.

John You glad you did the play?

George I am. Aye, I am. I am.

John You worked hard. You know how good you are. You know that.

George Get out.

John You are.

George I wish I could do more of it.

John You should try it. I've said.

George Don't be . . . No. Not to . . .

John Pete said.

George He did. He was being kind.

John You could.

George What's the use of talking about it? I couldn't.

John That way . . .

George No.

John We could . . .

George No, John. You've got to be different to me. You've got to be like the little Quaker lass played the Virgin Mary. She's going to acting school in London.

John But you're better than she is. Peter says she's suburban.

George What does that mean? She's got a lovely speaking voice. She's a nice little girl. Very confident. Good luck to her.

John You're more interesting.

George No.
Oh well. Come on. I'm going to bed. Coming?

John Well, we know what it is really, don't we?

George Do we?

John Well, we might as well say it. You can't leave, can you?

George No, I can't.

John I don't think it's because she's ill, see. I think it would be the same if she wasn't ill.

George Oh yeah? How do you make that out?

John I can tell.

George It's you always delving into things. I can't leave her now, can I? Well, can I? Aye? Whatever you say the reason is. Can I?

John No.

George Come on, sweetheart. We'll not solve anything tonight.

They go upstairs.

Four

A *few months later. Morning. George is alone. Arthur comes in.*

Arthur I thought you'd be up here.

George Yes.

Arthur Well, where else would you be?

George Aye.

Arthur I told Barbara you'd gone home. She wanted to be certain. I dunno where she'd think you'd go.

George I couldn't stay any longer, Arthur. I had enough. You know.

Arthur You don't have to tell me. I was glad to get out for a bit. Still, it went off well. Good turnout. Yes. Good crowd. Nice spread. I don't know what they'll do with all that food Barbara and she made. I wanted Barbara to let me get a drink in. But no. You know chapel people. Doreen said it wouldn't do and that. Still, they're not miserable. Said very nice things, you know, very nice.

George Aye.
I could do with a pint. Do you fancy a pint?

Arthur I do. I do. I don't think we'd better, though.

George I don't see why not.

Arthur Oh, you know what they'd say.

George Say what they like. I thought on that too. We could go over to Pickstead.

Arthur They'd still get news of it.

Jack comes in.

George Hello, Jack. You had too much of it, too?

Jack Aye.
(*to his father*) She wants you.
All right, George?

Arthur Are you going back down?

George No, I don't think so. Come for a drink?

Arthur No, I don't think so, George.
(*to Jack*) What does she want me for?

Jack I think they're saying goodbye to all the people.

Arthur Right.

George Aye, Arthur, they've had interest in your old cottage. People from Leeds. He's not selling. He's renting.

Arthur No, he'll not sell. He's not stupid. Selling property on his land.

Jack Leeds. I'd like to go to Leeds.

Arthur What, to work?

Jack Maybe.

George I thought when he helped with the harvest, he'd stay with us.

Arthur Aye. He'll have to find something soon. Won't you?

Jack Aye.

George Gaffer'll take him on.

Arthur Oh well, I'd better see what she wants. I'll miss her not being here. Your mother. I've know her all my life. In and out of here. All my life. Stayed here many a time. Well. (*He goes.*)

George How you managing?

Jack I've never been to a funeral. I was a bit scared. I didn't know what might happen. But it was all right.

George Hey, if you want the job he's willing to take you on, you know. He says he'll take someone on. Up to you, Jack.

Jack Good food.

George You'll be eating that for a week.
I'm going up later. Do you want to come?

Jack I dunno.
Never seen so much tea drunk.

George They like their tea. That's a stimulant.

Jack I didn't know most of the people.

George You know the people from the village.

Jack I know people from the village. All the relatives, I didn't know most of them.

George You know Frank and them.

Jack Oh aye, I know them. Well, I'm off then. All right?

George Where you going?

Jack I'm going into the village. All right?

Doreen comes in the back door.

Doreen It's me.

Jack Tara then.

George Think on, Jack. Jack!

Jack All right. See you later. I'll be up.

George Tara.

Doreen Jack.

Jack goes.

I'll not be long. I missed you leaving, that's all. I must help Barbara clear up. I just popped up. I wanted to see you were all right. For myself.

George I'm all right.

Doreen Anything you want me to do while I'm here.

George No, Doreen.

Doreen I don't mean to intrude, George. Am I intruding?

George No.

Doreen I'll go.

George What's the matter with you?

Doreen You don't want people crowding you. Time like this. I'll go. You want me to go.

George What do you mean, Doreen?

Doreen They all mean well, George.

George Course they all mean well. I know that. But what's that mean to me? Nothing. Nothing. All them flowers. Waste of brass.

Doreen Why are you so hard?

George I'm not.

Doreen Hard on yourself. They have to pay their respects. Barbara found it very comforting, I think.

I shall be lost without your mother. Oh, I'm filling up. Look. Oh dear.

George Nay. Doreen, don't. What is it?

Doreen It's you. You're so sad, I know you are. And I'm sad for you, George. And there's no comforting you. I can't comfort you, can I? I can't. Oh dear. I didn't mean to carry on like this. I just want you to take care of yourself.

George Why wouldn't I take care of myself? I've been looking after things all right these past months, haven't I?

Doreen You have. You have. I'm so sorry.

George I don't want anyone to take care of me, Doreen. Thank you. I don't mean to hurt anyone. I'm just glad it's over. I could only take so much. That's all. I'm all right here.

Barbara enters with a plate of food covered with a cloth.

Doreen Oo, Barbara. I hope you haven't been clearing up by yourself now.

Barbara No. Just brought these up for him.

George No. I don't want anything.

Barbara This'll keep, this. I've put it in here. All right? All right, George?

George Aye.

She comes into the living room.

Doreen They all gone?

Barbara Yes, they've all gone.

Doreen I'm just popping home, Barbara. I'll be back to help. Won't be long. (*Doreen goes.*)

Barbara What's the matter with Doreen?
I'm exhausted. You?

George No. I'm all right. She's just upset, I think.

Barbara I haven't taken it all in. Still. I'll go to the cemetery tomorrow.

George What for?

Barbara I'd like to. I didn't take it all in. Look at the flowers again. Didn't you see all the flowers out front?

George No. Not really.

Barbara Anyway, they all asked after you. As they went.

George I was there long enough, wasn't I?

Barbara Perhaps we should have done it up here. Would that have been better?

George No, Barbara.

Barbara She went from home. That's something.

George It's all right.

Barbara We'll have to arrange for the headstone to be done. Under Father's name.

George Oh Barbara, shut up will you?

Barbara Well, we'll have to think of these things.

George Father didn't have a headstone. Did he?

Barbara He did.
We'll have to sort her things.

George She didn't have anything. She didn't leave anything. Just enough to bury her.

Barbara She had you in that club, you know. You'll have to keep up the payments.

George No. You can throw me out with the ashes.

Barbara Don't, George. We'll have to sort her things.

George She didn't have anything.

Barbara No. But some of her clothes, some poor old people could do with them. That coat you bought her last winter. Doreen'll know someone. She never got the wear of it.

George I can't do it. I won't be doing it.
Look at this. (*He takes a box from the dresser.*)

Barbara What?

George Her savings book.

Barbara looks in the book.

Barbara Nothing in it. What did she keep it for?

George I don't know. It was in here with birth certificates and that – her marriage lines.

Barbara Just a penny in it to keep it open.

George There's her wedding ring. You have it now.

Barbara You keep it.

George I don't want anything.

Barbara You know you don't have to stay. You can do what you like now.

George Aye.

Barbara I had a nice card from your friend John. Did I tell you?

George Yes, you did.

Barbara Very nice. Should I send a letter back?

George I don't know.

Barbara Don't you stay in touch?

George Now and then.

Barbara There's nothing to keep you here, you know, George.

George No.

Barbara It's none of my business.

George No.

Barbara I'd like Dad's silver cup.

George OK.

Barbara What about Doreen?

George There's those heavy earrings.

Barbara She don't have pierced ears.

George Well, I don't know. Look, I'm going out, Barbara.

Barbara George, where you going?

George Up to work.

Barbara Today?

George Check a few things. Jack's coming later. I don't know if he'll stick it. We'll see.

George goes out. Doreen comes in.

Doreen All alone?

Barbara He's gone out for a walk. I think he wants to be on his own, Doreen.

Doreen Yes.

Barbara Well, it's hard for him.

Doreen And you, Barbara.

Barbara Oh yes. Oh yes. Well, we'll go. Thanks. Not a lot to do. We needed all those cups. Thank you.

Is there anything you want, Doreen, of Mother's? There isn't much.

Doreen No.

Barbara Well, if there is anything.

Doreen goes to the dresser.

Doreen There's this little thing. We bought it when we went over to Scarborough. Perhaps that.

Barbara Of course. Of course. Anything.

Doreen How will he manage?

Barbara He's quite self-sufficient, Doreen, you know.

Doreen Oh yes. But on his own. Will he manage?

Barbara Well, he will miss her. She was very fond of him, you see. I never minded. I didn't really.

Doreen They got on.

Barbara Yes. He's a solitary one. I think he's not someone for you, Doreen.

Doreen No.

Barbara I don't think he's for marrying, Doreen, you see.

Doreen No. I see that. I'll keep an eye on him, though.

Barbara Come on then. Shall we go?

Doreen Yes.

Mother comes in.

Barbara It's been an awful day for him.

Mother George?

Doreen And you.

Jack comes in.

Jack Nan!

Barbara Right, come on.

Arthur comes in.

Arthur Barbara.

Mother George.

John comes in with a carrier bag, dressed as in the first scene.

John I'm back.

They all go except for John.

George Is there a towel? Is there one there, John?

John Hang on. (*Finds towel.*) Yeah. Yes. Do you want it?

George comes in as he was in the first scene, when he went into the kitchen, but without a shirt.

George Where is it? Oo. Thanks.

John I bought you a shirt in 'Take Six'. Do you want to wear it?

George Oh, thanks. No, it's too good to wear tonight. Thanks. Good, there we are. Where's my clean jeans? Give me my jeans, kid.

He gives him his trousers.

John Thanks. Which shirt?

George Choose one.

John This is good. (*Gives him a shirt.*)

George OK. That's better. Thanks for this. It's great. Where's . . .

John Here we are. (*Hands him shoes.*)

George There we are.

John Yeah.

George Well. (*Looks at the jug of flowers on the table.*)

John These are nice flowers. Did you do these?

George Oh yeah. Doreen. You know Doreen. Very kind. She's been keeping my mother's little garden out there. Barbara ironed these shirts. I can't fend them off.

John You're all right, then?

George Yeah. I am.

John So you're managing, then?

George I'm managing fine. Is that all right?

John I was sorry to hear about your mother.

George You said.

John I didn't feel I should come.

George You could have come. No one would have minded. I'd have liked it.

John I'm sorry.

George No. No. Sorry.

John I thought of not coming tonight. You wouldn't have known. But I couldn't come to York and not see you. You wouldn't have known.

George Why did you come, then?

John You want your pound's worth, don't you?

George What do you mean?

John Don't.

George Well, you said make a break. A clean break.

John You can be hard.

George Aye. I can be hard. What about you? What are you? You're more compassionate, are you?
I think you are.

John Your mother liked me.

George I know. What you say that for?

John I don't know. I don't know.
Look at you. It's just looking at your . . . I can't. When I see your mouth and your hair. Oh please. Come back with me.

George Don't talk soft.

John I know. I know. Stupid.

George If you said jump in the lake, I'd do it. There's not much you couldn't make me do.

John Except what I want you to do.

George I couldn't do what you wanted me to. I had to come back.

John I know. I know. But it's different now. You can do what you like now.

George I couldn't. I couldn't live in London, me.

John You liked it.

George I did.

John There's nothing to keep you here. Is there?

George I live here. I live here. You can't see that, though. You can't see it. This is where I live. Here.

John You liked London.

George I did. I did. It was all right. It was great for a visit. All the visits. But what would I do? Where would I live? In your little room, sleeping in that three-quarter bed? I liked it. You know I did. They were all friendly, your friends. All of them.

And all the things to do. That we did. The picture galleries. That picture house on Oxford Street. The National Film Theatre. All the theatres and the concerts and the chat and everything. The white rooms and brass beds my mother said they had when she was a child. And the white Japanese lampshades and bookcases made out of bricks and planks. And the Whitechapel Gallery and American paintings and the deal tables and the bentwood chairs and the crocheted shawls.

And they were friendly. Very friendly people. Mad-heads, half of them. And the real coffee. Ugh. And the red wine, worse. And dinner in the night. I liked most of all that play on a Sunday. That was right good. Nearly a fight there was over that. What a lot they were. And the ballet. The ballet. Me. That curtain swinging up. All of it. And they were all nice too. And I enjoyed it all because you did. I'd do owt for you. But what would I do? Where would I work?

John Become an actor. I'd help you.

George I couldn't. It's too late, John.

John No.

George Listen to me speak.

John But that's all changed. I told you. Everything like that's changing. It's different. It's all going to be different. It's going to change. It's changing.

George Is it? I didn't see it. I couldn't learn to speak differently now. I couldn't be in Shakespeare, me. And if I couldn't do that! No. No thanks. Just be some Northerner as a job. Who'd let me do owt else? You know they wouldn't. I wouldn't blame them.
And I'd want to be more, whatever – wide-ranging. It's too late. I've left it too late. You got to be seventeen, eighteen, true. And, you know, I've got no . . . That's it. I'm not ambitious. You've got to be ambitious. I've none. I live here.

John But you're so good.

George That's what you say.

John It's true.

George No.

John It is. It is.

George You come up here. Come up here.

John I can't.

George Why not?

John You know I can't.

George Get a job in York in the theatre. Live here. Drive to York. Or Scarborough. Work from here. Rent Arthur's old cottage. No. No. Stupid. I'm stupid. See you light the kerosene lamp. Cook on a range. Keep a paraffin lamp in the lav. Get your bollocks frozen in winter having a shit outside. Have the pipes froze. Go down that lane in the slush. Cross that field to get to the village. Or move in here with me. Yeah. But how would we explain that? No. We'll have to let it go. See each when we can. As it was.

John Don't be such a bastard.

George Why? How? It was your choice. I was all right. You broke it off. Clean break, you said. All or nothing. Probably right. I thought we could leave it. Let it go as it went.

John We did.

George But it wasn't good enough for you.

John I couldn't just leave it to meet whenever and if.

George But that's what's happened. You came to York. You came over and I'm glad to see you. That's what's happened.

John I can't just let it be, drift apart. I don't feel casual about you. There was nothing casual about it. I haven't come for a fuck. It isn't casual sex. I've had plenty of casual sex.

George Shut up. Talking like that.

John It's all right for you.

George Aye.

John You've got it cosy up here. Tucked up by your sister and Doreen.

George She's all right, Doreen. She is. I like Doreen.

John Why don't you marry her?

George Perhaps I should.

John Better to marry than to burn.

George We're all right as it is.

John As what is?

George Doreen and me. We're sorted.

John Will you marry her then? Will you?

George Well, no. I dunno. I'm all right. Leave it, will you?

John So that's it.

George If you say so.

John I shouldn't have come.

George No.

John You're such a . . .

George What?

John Nothing.

George What? I'm such a what?

John George.

George It's got to be your way.

John No.

George Oh yeah? Why did you come?

John I know. I know. I'm sorry.

George I could fucking kill you.
Don't leave me.

John Come with me.

Doreen comes in.

Doreen Oo. You in?

John Oh Christ. I'm going.

George Fuck it. Don't go. Don't go.

Doreen Here we are.

George Look who's here.

Doreen Well, this is a surprise.

John Hello, Doreen.

Doreen You had your tea, George?

George No, not yet.

Doreen What brings you up here, John?

George He's in York with a play.

John Yes. I have to go. I've got to get back before curtain down.

George No.

Doreen Just for the week?

John Yes.

George Don't go yet.

Doreen We should try and see it, George.

George Aye.

John I must.

Doreen Have you directed it, John?

John Yes.

Doreen That's good. Will you put these in the shed for me, George? They're bulbs. I want to put them out.

George What do you want me to do?

Doreen Put these out there for me, will you?

George Aye, give 'em here. Won't be long. OK? (*George goes out.*)

Doreen So you here for a week? We haven't seen you for a long time. We thought you'd forgotten us. Got your work?

John Yes.

Doreen That's important.

John Yes. That's right. Look, I have to go.

Doreen No, surely you'll have a cup of tea?

John No.

Doreen Are you sure?
George! John's going. George!
He'll be in now. Sit and have tea with us.

John I'm late. I'll have to go. I'm going. OK? Goodbye. (*He goes.*)

Doreen George!

George comes in.

George What? Where's John?

Doreen He had to go.

George What? What do you mean? Why did you let him go?

Doreen You might catch him.

George goes out.

Look at this place. (*Begins to tidy up. Looks at the range.*) We'll have to take that out.

George comes in.

George I missed him.

Doreen You couldn't have. He'll be going for the bus.

George He's got a car.

Doreen Oh. I didn't know. You'll see him during the week.

George Yes.

Doreen I'll make you your tea. I got chops. You like them. (*She goes out.*)

George
Foxes their dens have they
Birds have their nests so gay
But the son of man this day
Has not where his head he may rest.

THE LOOK ACROSS THE EYES

For Bernard and Paul

Characters

Laurence, in his thirties

May, late forties

Jimmy, late forties

Harry, late forties

Young Laurence, sixteen

Christopher, eleven

David, eighteen

The play takes place in May and Harry's house in Cardiff, mainly in the late 1940s.

ONE

Laurence Jimmy Murphy was sitting hunched over the fire with the poker in his hand and a cup of tea near him handy in the grate. His sister, May Harrington, was ironing at the corner of the table. She used a flat-iron and she had folded a blanket, scorched and holed from use, into a square to protect the table.

May Stop poking the fire, Jimmy, for goodness' sake.

Jimmy You wanna put some coal on.

Harry Bring a few lumps.

Jimmy Haven't you got a bucket?

Harry Bring it on a shovel for now.

Laurence Jimmy picked up the shovel and went through the back kitchen outside to the coalhouse where, using a hammer, he broke a slab of coal into pieces, which he brought back in, piled on the shovel. He built the fire up.

Jimmy That'll need some small coal in a minute.

Laurence He went again to the back kitchen, this time to wash his hands and to dry them on the towel put out by May earlier. When he had finished he took a packet of sandwiches from the inside pocket of his overcoat hanging from a nail in the back door. He came back into the living room and took the sandwiches out of their brown paper-bag, which he folded carefully and put on the mantelpiece for May to use later. He reached into the inside pocket of his jacket, searching for a soiled envelope where he had put a pound note. He put it on the mantelpiece next to the paper bag. He sat down and began to toast the sandwiches on a copper toasting fork which May's eldest son, David, had made for her in work.

Jimmy She makes you sandwiches then.

Harry No, I bought them.

May For goodness sake, Jimmy, I'd make you a couple of sandwiches.

Jimmy Nah.

Laurence Jimmy had recently taken up lodgings in a boarding house near the docks run by a woman of whom May did not approve. For some years he had lived with an elderly cousin of theirs, where he had been comfortable and well cared for, but advancing years and the death of her husband had forced the old lady to give up her little house and move in with her daughter. May wasn't happy with the present arrangements. Jimmy had no experience of looking after himself. It wasn't expected of him. For ten years after their mother's death, until her marriage, May had kept house for him in town, where they had been born. They were the youngest of ten children with barely a year between them and although May was the younger of the two, it had never appeared to be so to anyone else.

May Do you want any dinner? There's enough.

Jimmy No.

May Are you sure, Jimmy? You're getting as thin as a rake. Look at you.

Laurence She stopped ironing and went over to him.

May Let me look at you.

Jimmy Get off.

May Hold still. Let me look at you.

Laurence She inspected him as she would one of her children.

May Look at your neck. You could do with a good wash and all. Look at the inside of your collar.

Jimmy Gor blimey. Mind your own business. It's my working shirt.

Laurence May left him and went back to the ironing.

May And don't let my fire burn up, there's a fuel shortage.

Jimmy You wanna get a bucket.

May Kiss my . . .

Laurence Jimmy picked up the shovel and went outside to do as he was told. May tested the iron by holding it near her cheek, only to find that the heat was gone out of it. She put it upright on the table and stood for a while, supporting her back with her right hand. She went into the back kitchen to change irons. She wanted to finish one more shirt before her husband and sons came in to dinner. The back kitchen still had a range, which she no longer used for cooking but which was sufficiently heated by the fire in the other room to boil a kettle or heat her flat irons or air the clothes on a wooden airer, hoisted and lowered by means of a pulley fastened to a cleat on the side of the dresser.

She turned from the old range to the gas cooker on which she was making the dinner. Sunday's lamb had lasted them two days and this morning she had used the bone to make a thick soup with potatoes and onions and pearl barley. It was simmering now on the stove in a big pan. She stirred it and tasted it and when she was satisfied she looked into the saucepan next to it, where were steaming dumplings, which she had made from suet and flour. This was a favourite meal with them and since they would eat their bread dry with the soup there would be no grumbling about margarine from the boys today. Jimmy came in with the small coal. May turned from the cooker and, protecting her hand with a piece of flannel and the end of her apron, she picked up the hot iron and went into the other room, where Jimmy was putting the small coal on the fire. May went on with the ironing. Jimmy began to eat one of his sandwiches.

May You'd better move in with us, I think.

Jimmy I'd watch it.

Laurence She spat lightly on the iron, which sizzled loudly, and having measured the heat, she began to iron the shirt, carefully.

Jimmy Blimey, it's hot in here.

May Well, take your coat off.

Jimmy Nah.

May You've gone a contrary bugger, our Jimmy.

Jimmy I'll be going in a minute. You've gone a terrible woman for swearing.

May It's you, God forgive me. You've got me heart scalded.

Jimmy You never hear me swear.

Laurence She never did.

Jimmy Not like him.

Laurence Jimmy nodded his head towards the house next door.

Jimmy He's got a mouth on him.

May Who?

Jimmy Next door, Tommy Ryan.

May Is he home?

Jimmy Yes, I just saw him out there.

May Isn't he working?

Jimmy He was working this morning. He was picked out all right. Must have been a soft job.

Laurence Jimmy and Tommy Ryan had stood in the pen with the other dockers early that morning under the scrutiny of the docks manager. Jimmy hadn't been picked to work again. He had taken his book to be stamped in the office and then cycled over to May. Whether it was his poor sight, or past militancy, or religion, or whatever it was that worked against him, he did not know. It was something.

Jimmy Well, they was never any good.

May Who?

Jimmy Them.

May Who?

Jimmy Tommy Ryan, all of them.

May What are you talking about?

Jimmy Him next door. They used to live in Mary Ann Street. That was a rough house.

May Don't talk daft, Jimmy, he comes from right down by Adeline Street. Lived down the bottom from Harry.

Jimmy They never did.

May They did. The ones you mean were cousins of his.

Jimmy I went to school with one of them. He was in my class.

May I know. I know.

Jimmy Well, how could you know better than me?

May Because you was bloody backward then and you're bloody backward now.

Jimmy Well that's nice. (*He chuckles.*)
Well, we'll wait till Harry comes in and see who's right.

May Shut up will you, for God's sake. I'm sick of your voice.

Jimmy We'll wait till Harry comes. He'll know. Where is he?

May I give him a tanner for a bet.

Jimmy Has he had any compo through?

May No.

Jimmy He'll never get any. It's a waste of time with them people.

Laurence Harry had contracted a skin disease in his youth. For years it had been in remission but during the war, soon after he was conscripted, it had flared up again when May had lost her baby. It was so bad now that he couldn't work.

May I don't know what she sees in him.

Jimmy Who?

May Her next door.

Jimmy Oh yeah.

May She thinks he's Clark Gable.

Jimmy Does she?

Laurence She stopped ironing for a moment.

May It's the rent man today.

Jimmy You plays a different tune now.

May Yerra, you mean old get. Keep it. His hands are in a shocking state again. Nothing'll shift it.

Jimmy I don't know why he give up the dock. God, he was a blue-eye down there. I've been down there since I was fourteen. I've never had a quarter of the jobs he used to get.

May Aye, well, what we all should have done and it wouldn't matter where he was now, would it? And his skin was ruined from working as a lagger in the channel dry dock. He was years in the dry dock right after he left school.

Jimmy You can't see them admitting to that. Has the ship's owners' doctor been?

May They sent someone here last week. He came in a little cream sports car, with the hood down. It's going to drag on and on.

Jimmy I can never see it coming off. He never had any right to a book anyway.

May Where?

Jimmy On the docks.

May He did you know. Bloody cheek.

Jimmy He did not.

May He bloody did. His father was an iron ore man.

Jimmy Get out.

May Look, see this.

Laurence She brandished the iron at him. He chuckled again and got up to make ready to leave. May finished ironing the shirt. She folded it and put it with the others ready to be aired, on the deep window-ledge behind her. She would do what little remained tomorrow or at the end of the week. She folded the blanket and put it away in the cupboard and then she took the iron into the kitchen.

Jimmy Where's my clips?

Laurence May came back in and began to lay the table for dinner.

May Well, where did you put them?

Laurence She left the table and went over to the fireplace.

May Here they are. They were on the mantelpiece. If they were a dog they'd bite you.

Laurence She found the pound Jimmy had put out earlier. She kissed it.

Jimmy That's all you think about is money.

Laurence Jimmy put his clips on.

May On your way, brother. I'll give it to you on Friday.

Laurence She put the pound in the rent book. The back door opened. May's second son, Laurence, came in from school.

Jimmy Aye, aye.

Laurence Jimmy went out. Laurence said nothing.

May What's the matter with you?

Young Laurence Nothing's the matter with me.

May Something's the matter with you.

Laurence Laurence had failed in one subject to get his school certificate. May and Harry had insisted on his staying on at school for another year to resit his exams. He didn't want to. He didn't want to.

Young Laurence What's for dinner?

May Hang on, hang on, take your blazer off. Sit down.

Laurence Laurence took his blazer off and put it on the back of the chair. He sat down. May went into the kitchen and brought him his soup.

Young Laurence Aren't there any doughboys?

May Wait a minute, wait a minute.

Laurence She went back into the kitchen to fetch the dumplings. She gave him two.

Young Laurence Great.

May Yes. You've cheered up now, see.

Young Laurence Yes.

May What d'you do in school?

Laurence Laurence didn't answer. Jimmy came back in.

Jimmy Where's Harry's pump? I got a flat tyre.

May Out there.

Laurence Jimmy went out grumbling to himself as David and Christopher, May's other two sons, came in. David and Jimmy had seen each other that morning in the docks. David was an apprentice welder. Christopher, the youngest, had recently passed the scholarship and was in the same school as Laurence. David had given him a lift home on the back of his bike.

Christopher Hello, Mam. What's for dinner?

May You'll see. It's your favourite. You don't look too bright either. What's the matter with the pair of you?

David I'm all right. I don't know about him.

Christopher And I'm all right too.

May I know you're all right. Come on then, sit down.

David I'd better wash my hands first.

Laurence He went into the kitchen. May followed him. Christopher sat at the table next to Laurence.

May (*to David*) What's the matter?

Laurence David dried his hands.

David I'm all right, Mam.

May I don't know.

David I'm all right, honest.

Laurence He went back in and sat down. May ladled soup into two plates, added two dumplings to each of them and brought them in.

Christopher Can't I have a big plate?

May No, I'm keeping the other big plate for your father. That'll do you.

Laurence Oh, Mam.

May Come on now, there's plenty. Come on now.

Laurence Jimmy came in again.

Jimmy It's no good, I must have a puncture. I'll have to take Harry's bike. He won't mind.

May No. Now go on. Go on.

Jimmy Gor blimey.

May Yes, I know. I'll see you tomorrow.

Laurence Jimmy went out.

Christopher Have you made enough doughboys for afters?

May You haven't finished your dinner yet.

Laurence She had made enough doughboys for afters, and when they had finished the soup she cleared the plates and brought them each a doughboy on a plate with jam to sweeten it.

Young Laurence Yeah.

David Thanks.

Christopher Great.

May I'll make tea when your father comes in.

Laurence When they had finished eating, Christopher went out to play and Laurence went upstairs to read. David sat by the fire.

David That was lovely, Mam.

May Did you like it?

David Lovely.

Laurence May cleared the table.

David I'll do that.

May No, I'll do it, you sit down, you must be tired.

David I am.

Laurence Harry came in as May was setting a place for him.

Harry I see Jim got my bike.

May He's got a slow puncture.

Harry He didn't see me.

May How did you do on the horses?

Harry Hopeless. Hello, son.

May Are you telling me the truth?

Harry Of course I am.

May Look at me. You bloody big liar.

Laurence She hit him. He laughed.

Harry Mine came up.

May What was the odds?

Harry Five-to-two. There's your tanner. I bought five Park Drive, OK?

Laurence He gave her a kiss and her sixpence.

May Give old cheerful Charlie one, for Christ's sake.

Harry Cor blimey.

Laurence He tossed David a cigarette.

David Thanks.

Laurence He lit his cigarette from the fire.

May Don't do that.

Laurence Harry lit his cigarette from David's and then handed it back.

May And before you sit down to dinner, go and do your hands. Come on.

Harry I reckon I'm doing them too much.

May I don't know. Here they are, ironed and aired.

Laurence She gave him clean, rolled-up bandages for his hands. She had washed them that morning.

Harry Ta.

Laurence With his cigarette in his mouth he began to unknot the bandages at his wrist.

May Shall I do them?

Harry I'll manage.

May Listen what a flutter does for him. You're a different fella, isn't it terrible? That's the devil in you.

Harry Aye.

Laurence Harry went upstairs to their bedroom, where the cream was for his hands. May turned to David.

May Don't go to sleep, David, come on. You'll have to go back to work soon. Come on.

David All right.

May Come on.

David In a minute.

May David.

Laurence David didn't respond. May stood looking at him. Then she turned and called to Harry upstairs.

May Aye, Harry.

Harry Yes?

May I think our Jim'll have to move in with us.

Laurence She waited.

May Did you hear?

Harry Yes.

Laurence Harry came in, having put on the clean bandages.

Harry Tie these for me, will you?

Laurence May tied the bandages carefully. Harry sat down at the table.

May He looks awful uncared for.

Harry Where we going to put him?

May Well, Jimmy can have Christopher's bedroom, or he can go in with the boys.

David Christ.

Harry Well, please yourself.

May Anyway, it'll be a help.

Harry Yeah.

May Well, how do you think the rent is going to be paid today?

Harry I haven't said anything.

May You never do. All right, we'll let the poor bugger stick where he is.

Harry Please yourself. It's nothing to do with me. Any dinner, Mother?

May Look I've told you often enough, don't talk to me in that bloody stupid way.

Harry All right. All right. All right.

May Do you know, I'll knife you before we're much older.

Harry You've been going to do that ever since we met, my dear. You got a big mouth.

May Yerra, you're as common as they come.

David Shut up.

May What did you say?

David I'm going back to work.

May You haven't had a cup of tea yet.

David That's OK.

Laurence He kissed his mother and went out. May went into the kitchen to get Harry's dinner. She brought it back and set the plate down before him.

Harry What's the matter with David?

May Don't ask me now. I expect we'll hear it all Friday when he brings his pay packet in. He doesn't want to finish his time.

Harry Well, that's stupid talk, isn't it?

May Well, don't talk to him in a tone of voice like that. You've got no manner of talking.

Harry Don't worry, my dear, I shan't say a word.

May Yerra, you're an ignorant bloody get, you are.

Laurence Laurence came down.

Young Laurence I'm going back to school.

May You're early.

Young Laurence Yeah.

May Will you take Christopher with you?

Young Laurence No I won't. He's big enough.

May Well call him in when you go.

Laurence Laurence put on his blazer, picked up his books and kissed his mother before going back to school. He went through the back door.

Young Laurence Christopher!

May I don't know what's the matter with the pair of them.

Harry Well, I think we should have taken him away and put him to a trade.

May It's only the one subject. It's only French. He's champion at everything else. He've got to have a language.

Harry Don't they teach another language?

May No. Or, well . . . not in his class.

Laurence Christopher ran in.

May Go and wash.

Christopher Mam.

May Go and wash.

Laurence He went into the kitchen and washed his hands and face. He came back in.

May Come here. Look at you.

Laurence She cleaned his mouth with the end of her apron.

Christopher Don't.

May There we are. Go on. Go on.

Laurence Christopher kissed his mother and ran out.

Harry He's no bother.

May No, he's no bother.

Laurence Harry pushed his plate away.

Harry Mother, that was great.

TWO

Laurence Later that night Harry was sitting by the fireplace in his pyjamas. The fire had long since gone out. His hands prevented him from clearing the ashes or laying the fire. Perhaps David would do it in the morning. He was the first up. May came in wearing her nightdress with a cardigan over it. She was barefoot.

May What's the matter, can't you sleep?

Laurence He shook his head.

May Your nerves bad?

Harry Shocking.

May Oh, Harry.

Harry Now leave me alone, there's a good girl.

May You're a silly man. You're very silly to be like this. Come back to bed.

Harry Go on, I'll be up.

Laurence He had been like this now for nearly four years, ever since he had been invalided out of the army because of his hands, and on compassionate grounds because she had lost the baby. She went back to the war in her mind.

May They should never have called a man your age up.

Harry Don't be silly, May.

May Well, what bloody use were you going to be to them. It half-killed me at home here. And if I hadn't lost the baby, they'd never have let you out and then you'd have been over there.

Harry That's no way to look at it.

May We don't know what would have happened. You might have been killed. You might have. Then you wouldn't have come home. How do you think I felt?

Harry Don't keep on.

May Feel.

Harry Shut up will you. It's got nothing to do with it. It was my hands.

May I will not shut up. I don't think it was really so bad. I really don't. To me it's not those things that harden you. It's wicked to let the death of children harden you when you've got other children. There's so much more preventable to make you hard. Look at it that way.

Harry You don't know what it's like being on the touchline of these things.

May No? But I do, you know. Carrying a baby. Whether you really want it or not, but you think, well, it's God's will and you can't but look forward I should think, not if it's your twentieth. And then there's nothing and no explanation given. You don't feel in the thick of things. Let me tell you. Look at you. You're like six penn'orth of bad ha'pennies. I felt. You can't imagine it. Oh, it's a terrible feeling.

Laurence Harry remembered the night he came home from the army and how long it had taken to cross the country.

Harry God, it was pouring down. And the blackout, and no trains. It was comical it was so depressing.

Laurence They both laughed.

May Listen.

Laurence They both looked up.

May He've got out of the boys' bed now, and he's got into ours again.

Laurence Christopher travelled from bed to bed like this most nights.

May Go up and tell him to go back.

Harry He'll wake the bloody house up. Leave him. Leave him.

Laurence When he was fifteen, Harry's oldest sister Violet had lost her first child at birth. It was during the First War, in the winter of 1917, and her husband Tom was at the front. He'd gone in to see her as soon as he was allowed. Popped his head round the door and said.

Harry Hello, Vi.

Laurence She turned to look at him, smiling because she was so fond of him, but he was struck by her eyes, which were not smiling. How are you? he'd said, not knowing what else to say. I'm all right, love, how are you? Vi had said.

He looked into May's eyes now. They were different from Vi's, less simple, more acute. Less soft, less pitiable, less disconsolate, more bright, more forgiving, more clever, more kind, more arresting, more unnerving, more inconsolable. His boys had this look across their eyes. So had Jimmy, although his eyes were failing.

Years later, ten years, fifteen, Harry would come into this room. This room where they were sitting now silent.

He would come in to find Jimmy sitting by the fire reading a folded newspaper, lengthwise, near his eyes.

Harry What are you reading with no light on for, Jimmy? You haven't got no sight as it is. You're getting childish, Jimmy. Who did your sandwiches?

Jimmy I did. I was going to the match. They kept me waiting over an hour.

Harry Have you had any dinner?

Jimmy Nah.

Harry I expect Laurence put something ready for you out there.

Jimmy I dunno.

Harry Did you get your money?

Jimmy Aye. You had a bet?

Harry No.

Jimmy That'll be the day.

Harry I had a two bob double.

Jimmy What?

Harry The favourite, the first race, and I had a tip for the four o'clock.

Jimmy You always back the blinkin' favourite.

Harry Look, I've had a bet on every dinnertime for over going on sixty-odd years.

Jimmy They come up?

Harry One of them did.

Jimmy Which one?

Harry The favourite.

Jimmy Mug's game.

Harry Aye, I must be a mug to be still going out to work at my age.

Jimmy You must be doing all right on it.

Harry Look at you. You wanna get some exercise. I haven't turned into a bloody old-age pensioner like you. I saw someone helping you across the road last night.

Jimmy Couldn't have been me.

Harry You couldn't see me, though.

Jimmy I must have been helping them.

Harry Well, it was the blind leading the blind then.

Laurence His hands would be cured by then. David would have finished his trade by then, he would be married with children of his own by then, with a house and a mortgage. I would fail my exam again, but my grammar school education would have got me a job in the council offices, I would still be living at home. Christopher would have gone to university and be living away and would rarely come home. I would have come in from work. Hello, unc, I would have said.

Jimmy What? Oh aye. You all right?

Laurence Had your tea?

Jimmy What?

Laurence Had your tea? I put it up for you.

Jimmy Nah. I'm all right.

Laurence I'll get it for you, shall I?

Jimmy Aye, all right.

Laurence Where's Dad?

I would have got him his tea. May would be dead by then. Things would be different by then. May would be dead by then. But now Harry and May were sitting with each other in the night, and they had no understanding that after this things would change between them and that she would lose strength and that he would get better.

May Come on. Let's go up.

Harry All right.

Laurence They went upstairs and got into bed and went to sleep with their youngest boy between them.

THREE

Laurence The next day, Jimmy was sitting by the fire, the paper close to his eyes. May poured him a cup of tea.

May Your sight's getting worse, Jimmy. Why don't you get glasses?

Jimmy Nah.

May Oh well.

Jimmy I've brought Harry's bike back. I'll have to mend my puncture. I wonder if David have got a patch.

May His puncture kit's out there. You'd better ask him though.

Jimmy Aye.

May You eaten today?

Jimmy Aye, aye.

Laurence Jimmy looked tired, she thought.

May What work you been on?

Jimmy I been working on the Glasgow.

May Oh dear.

Laurence The Glasgow was a coaster which came into Cardiff every two weeks. On alternate weeks it went over to Dublin. It was the most hated boat on the dock. The cargo was always unwieldy and couldn't be moved by crane. It always took a long time to unload and so it was poorly paid. Today it had brought loose timber, none of it lashed.

May Oh dear.

Laurence She gave him his tea. Jimmy put the cup in the grate.

Jimmy I'd better move in with you I think.

May I'd watch it.

Laurence Said May. How they loved each other.

LOVELY EVENING

For Rose

Characters

Harry

Laurence

Jimmy

Neighbour

Marion

Waiter

The play takes place in Cardiff
in the early 1950s.

ONE

Harry Lovely evening. I say, lovely evening.

Laurence It was. It was a lovely evening. It had been a lovely day and now it was a lovely evening. And there were children outside playing in the street and there were swallows flying low over the roofs and in the distance the sound of an ice-cream van and in the park they would be playing bowls and baseball. No, they wouldn't be playing baseball. If there was a baseball match my father would have said. But there might be a couple of people playing tennis in the old tennis courts and the swimming baths would still be open and there would certainly be kids on the swings and kids playing in the empty bandstand. And all over the city I dare say there would be people like my father and my uncle getting ready to go out because it was such a lovely evening. Not that the weather really had much to do with why either of them was going out. It was Wednesday and my father went to Benediction on Wednesdays and then to a meeting of one of his sodalities and after that for a pint. My uncle went out every evening whatever the weather was like. Rain, hail or sleet, he still went out. It would take something to keep him in. But still it was a lovely evening and it made the going out easy.

Harry Get cold later, mind, I should think. You going out later, Laurence?

Laurence I certainly was going out.
I don't know, Dad. I might later. I don't know.

Harry You going out I'd wear a jacket. I wouldn't go out in my shirt sleeves.

Laurence I certainly wouldn't go out in my shirtsleeves.

I was going to wear my new gaberdine trousers and my sports coat and a white shirt open over the collar of my jacket.

My father had his foot on the side of a chair and was brushing his shoe. My uncle was peering into the mirror over the fireplace, fastening his collar.

Jimmy Where's my stud? Where's my back stud? You had my back stud, Harry?

Harry I don't know where your stud is. I don't wear unattached collars.

Jimmy Where'd I put that, now? Gor blimey. Seen my stud, Laurence?

Laurence Let's see. Here it is.

It was on the mantelpiece, lying at the foot of the statue of Our Lady of Lourdes. At least he hadn't cut himself shaving.

Jimmy Thank you.

Harry There we are. You want these, Jimmy?

Jimmy Aye. Gimme the soft brush. I don't need polish.

Harry Make sure you put it out there after. Where you going anyway?

Jimmy What you want to know where I'm going?

Laurence Every evening he went out and every evening my father asked him where he was going. Just as my mother had always done. And every evening he didn't say. It was as if they were keeping faith with her by this ritual. She certainly would have asked him where he was going. And he certainly wouldn't have told her.

It was the same with my brothers and me when they were still at home. She'd quiz them. All of us. Me. 'Where you going, Laurence?' she would say. 'Out.' 'Where out?' 'Out.' 'Where?' 'Out, Mam. I'm going out.' She always knew where my father was going and if she didn't he'd tell if asked. But she usually knew where he was going. As we did tonight.

Harry There's Confession tonight, Laurence.

Jimmy Yes.

Laurence I wish I'd been to Confession. Only without having to go. But how could I say, 'I'm sorry for what I've done, but I'm afraid I know I'm going to do it again'? I wished he hadn't brought it up. I wish he'd go out so I could forget about it.

Harry Ttt. Well I'm off. Lock the back door if you're going out. You going out?

Laurence I don't know.

Harry Have you got your key, Jimmy?

Jimmy Aye.

Harry And put the shoe brush out there. Tara. Tara. I won't be late.

Jimmy There we are. I want a raincoat, Laurence?

Laurence No, it's not going to rain.

Jimmy Right. Do you want this?

Laurence Aye. I might. Give it to me.

Jimmy OK. There we are. Tara.

Laurence Tara.

When he had gone I too prepared to go out. First I cleaned my shoes, then I went upstairs to wash and change, and when I came down I checked my hair carefully in the mirror, then took a clean handkerchief from the pile on the window-ledge, locked the back door, got my raincoat and went out.

Woman's Voice All going out tonight, Laurence?

Laurence Aye.

Woman's Voice It's a lovely evening.

Laurence I walked down to Willows Avenue and got the bus into town.

TWO

Marion What have you brought a raincoat for?

Laurence It might rain.

Marion It won't rain.

Laurence Won't it?

Marion Silly.

Laurence Not so silly. I might need it.

Marion What for?

Laurence You never know.

Marion I've only brought a cardigan in case.

Laurence Well, I've only brought a raincoat in case.

We had met in the little park opposite the museum planted to commemorate the Welsh National Eisteddfod which had been held in Cardiff in nineteen-whenever, 1920-something. The garden was pretty in a tight and tidy sort of a way. In the centre was a circle of red granite stones like a miniature Stonehenge, recalling the

Eisteddfod's druidical past. And nearby stood a statue of Lord Ninian Crichton Stuart who fell at the Battle of Loos and who had been Cardiff's M.P. Aristocratic, Scottish, Tory, Catholic. And nearby too, and more appropriate, was a statue of John Cory, coal owner and philanthropist.

Marion What did you want to meet here for? I've never been here before.

Laurence I dunno. A change. Different, more private. You must have been here before.

Marion I haven't.

Laurence You must have walked through it when you've been to the museum.

Marion Not that I remember.

Laurence Do you want to sit down?

Marion No. I want to look first. It's pretty, isn't it? Look at that statue first. What's it say?

Laurence Lord Ninian Edward Crichton Stuart. M.P. for Cardiff, Cowbridge and Llantrisant. Lieutenant-Colonel, Sixth Battalion, Welch Regiment. 15th May 1883. Fell in France at the Battle of Loos fighting bravely for his country, 2nd October 1915.

Marion Ninian. There's a name. Ninian.

Laurence Ninian didn't seem an odd name to me. Ninian. I was in school with an Aelred, an Ambrose and five Michael Collinses.

Marion These must be old, these stones. Here.

Laurence Nah. They're mocky.

Marion They're not. They're real. They're real stones.

Laurence But they're not old.

Marion Why are they in a circle? What are they for? What are they meant to be?

Laurence They're meant to be an ancient place of worship, of sacrifice.

Marion Are they? Oo.

Laurence Yeah. That's where they would have sacrificed virgins at dawn. In there.

Marion Oh no.

Laurence Yeah. They would have. Would you have liked to be sacrificed at dawn?

Marion No, I wouldn't.

Laurence Would you like me to sacrifice you in them stones?

Marion No. Now. There's people.

Laurence You would. You'd love it.

Marion Now I'm warning you.

Laurence What?

Marion You know.

Laurence Know what?

Marion You know.

Laurence No. What?

Marion Stop it.

Laurence What?

Marion Laurence.

Laurence Why won't you let me?

Marion I'm not going to let you do anything here.

Laurence I know. But why won't you ever?

Marion Now don't start all that. You go far enough as it is.

Laurence You'd like it.

Marion Well whether I would or not, you're not going to find out.

Laurence If you liked me you would.

Marion If you liked me you wouldn't ask. And what would you think of me if I did?

Laurence I'd think you were a real woman.

Marion Oh aye. You'd think I was common. That's what you'd think.

Laurence I wouldn't. I wouldn't.

Marion No. I don't think you would. But there we are.

Laurence I'd be careful.

Marion You're not going to get a chance to be careful. Are you going to sulk?

Laurence No.

Marion You are. I'm going if you're going to be like this again.

Laurence I'm sorry. I'm sorry.

Marion Come on. Let's sit down. There have to be limits, Laurence.

Laurence Don't there?

Marion What's that supposed to mean?

Laurence Nothing.

Marion You think I'm stupid.

Laurence I don't. I think you're far from stupid.

Marion You see. You're a pig, you are.

Laurence All right. Calm down. Calm down. I know. I know.

Marion What's the matter with you, eh?

Laurence Nothing.

Marion There is.

Laurence Oh, I'm fed up.

Marion Are you?

Laurence Yeah.

Marion What with? With me?

Laurence Not with you. Don't be silly. Not with you.

Marion What with?

Laurence I don't know. Work. Yeah. I'm fed up with it. I don't want to be clerking for the council. The money's rubbish anyway. I'm packing it in. I am.

Marion Don't be silly. It's a good job. The hours are good.

Laurence Is it? Are they?

Marion What else are you going to do?

Laurence I don't know.

Marion Go to sea?

Laurence Oh. Aye.
You don't like it there, do you?

Marion It's all right. Yes. I do. Yeah.

Laurence Well, I don't. What do you want to do?

Marion Well, let's sit here for a bit now we're here.

Laurence Do you want to go to the pictures?

Marion No, I don't want to go to the pictures. Not on a lovely evening like this, I don't.

Laurence Well, what do you want to do then?

Marion I don't know. What's the hurry? What do you want to do?

Laurence Ah well.

Marion Don't start again.

Laurence Let's go for a drink.

Marion What?

Laurence Yeah. Come on.

Marion No.

Laurence Why not?

Marion I'm not going into a public house.

Laurence Why?

Marion Because I'm not. I wouldn't mind sitting outside somewhere.

Laurence Where?

Marion We could get a bus somewhere.

Laurence Ah. No. What's the difference between having half a shandy sitting outside the Carpenter's Arms on Rummy Hill and having half a shandy in Hallinan's? What's the difference?

Marion All the difference. It's nice out there. It's in the country.

Laurence Rummy Hill the country! Anyway, I don't want to go all the way back out there. We're in town now.

Marion We'll go for a coffee later.

Laurence Great.

Marion My mother wants to know when you're coming to tea again.

Laurence Oh dear. Does she?

Marion Don't be like that.

Laurence Like what?

Marion You know. She likes you.

Laurence Does she? I don't think she does.

Marion How do you make that out? She says you're a nice boy. But she says this is all hole-and-corner and you're not serious.

Laurence And she doesn't think I'm good enough for you.

Marion What makes you say that?

Laurence Of course she didn't think I was good enough for her. Fair dos. She was her mother. What else was she supposed to think? What would my mother have thought of her? Aye. Yeah. Well, she would have liked her. She would have thought she was a nice girl. She would have liked her because she was pretty and sweet and affectionate and no contender. 'Why can't you go out with a nice girl like that?' she would have said. Until you did. It was a matter of principle. She thought my father was a stranger enough in our lives without girls. 'He's going out with some girl,' she would say. How my brother David managed it to the altar, I don't know. Christopher had gone to university and never brought a girl home. Serious. Why did she want to bring serious into it? Why did she want me to go there to tea? I didn't want to go there to tea. All that. I didn't want to take two buses up the Heath. It was like a foreign country. I couldn't manage it. Any of it. The salad cream. The lincrusta. The red-hot pokers. The fourteen-inch television. The chair-back covers. The dining suite. The Festival of Britain curtains in the front room. In the lounge. It was all . . . I couldn't manage it. The china statue of the lady in the long dress holding her skirt out stranding on the window-ledge facing the street. It was too strange. Especially the statue of the lady in the long dress. There were many statues like that in the windows of houses like that. Boys holding bunches of grapes. Coy little girls. And other ladies in long dresses dancing or with their skirts ruffled in the wind, holding Afghan hounds on leads. My mother had a particular dislike for them. She was quite violent in her dislike. I think she saw them as graven images and in retaliation she put a chipped plaster statue of the Sacred Heart in our front-room window like a sign of faith or a statement of content over form. When it came to religious objects, taste was beside the point. And beauty was in short supply in the Catholic Truth Society. But in other matters, had she the cash she would have been for the modern, not the contemporary. And apart from the sparkling windows and the standard of housekeeping, she would have found it all as alien as I did.

Marion Will you?

Laurence Don't go on. Eh? Do you want to go for a walk?

Marion All right. Where shall we go?

Laurence Do you want to go into the castle grounds?

Marion OK.

THREE

Laurence She put her arm in mine and we walked out of the gardens and made our way to the great park of Cardiff Castle, past the Museum and City Hall, past Lord Tredegar on his horse, past Lloyd George brandishing his fist, and past, below us, the Marquess of Bute, Lord Ninian's father, standing in his own little garden. We went through East Gate, past the stables and the tennis courts, past the high walls of the castle gardens, over which we could see the derelict Norman keep on its mound, above the moat which was full of water lilies and beyond that we could see the clock tower, the centrepiece of this last eccentric throw of Victorian Gothic built by Lord Ninian's father who had been, my father said, as rich as any oil sheik and who had ruled over the growth of the city like a prince and whose name was everywhere recorded. And whose family had now retreated from the city and South Wales, realising its assets over the years and finally disposing of the castle and its grounds by way of a gift to the people and retreated to Scotland, declining from sultanate riches into mere wealth. In the freedom of the park she took my hand as if making a claim and a promise. I slipped my finger through hers so as to close the deal, whatever that was. We walked alongside the feeder canal, the black water diverted from the Taff above Black Weir flowing through the park and underground now most of its way, through town to fill the old docks. We stopped by a folly built like a pagoda with a bridge over the water.

Marion I don't like it, do you?

Laurence I don't know. It's all right.

Marion I don't like it.

Laurence I watched her looking at it, in her cotton dress and white sandals.
I was serious.

Marion Don't.

Laurence Come on.

Marion No. Look. People.

Laurence Please.

Marion Don't, you're hurting me.

Laurence Sorry. Sorry.

Marion I should think so.

Laurence Please.

Marion You're hurting me.

Laurence Am I?

Marion Yes.

Laurence Am I?

Marion Stop it.

Laurence Oh.

Marion Come here.

Laurence She took my hand and led me to the grove of shrubs, rhododendrons, masses of them, masses, all in bloom, all coloured red, in the middle of the park.

Marion They won't last much longer. Look.

Laurence She picked up a bright red petal from the ground.

Marion Here.

Laurence Red.
Please.

Marion No. There are people.

Laurence There aren't.

Marion I can hear them.

Laurence Come, let's go into the trees.

Marion Shall we?

Laurence Yes.

Marion I might ruin my dress.

Laurence Why do you think I brought a raincoat?

FOUR

Marion Am I all right?

Laurence Yes. What do you mean?

Marion Is my skirt marked?

Laurence Turn round.
No, you're fine. I told you I'd need my raincoat.

Marion Where's my compact? Oh. Here it is. Look at you.

Laurence What's the matter? What you laughing at?

Marion You've got lipstick all over your face. Give me your handkerchief.

Laurence No.

Marion Come on.

Laurence Look, you don't want it.

Marion Oo. Sticky.

Laurence I told you. Give it to me. Give me your mirror. Blimey.

Marion Yes.

Laurence Lend me your comb. God, I'm gorgeous.

Marion Give it back.

Laurence Come on then.

Marion Hang on. Do I look all right?

Laurence We walked back through the park near the trees.

Marion You're quiet.

Laurence I'm all right.

Marion Why are you laughing?

Laurence Nothing.

I was thinking of the first time I'd been to Confession after going out with a girl and having impurity to confess. And how I'd gone into the confessional not knowing how to tell my awful sin. 'Pray, father. Give me your blessing for I have sinned,' I said. 'Hello, Laurence. How's your mother?' he replied. I was too shocked to make a break so I stayed and lied by omission, confessing such venial sins that I wondered why he wasn't on to me. I'd never been able to confess anything like it since and I was case-hardened now in the knowledge that I was certainly facing damnation if I didn't rectify matters. What if I dropped dead? Sacrilege was a terrible sin.

We turned left out of the West Gate and went to look at the long wall over the top of which at intervals were stone animals with yellow glass eyes, seeming to swarm over it.

Marion I don't like them.

Laurence I do.

Marion What's that?

Laurence A lynx. It's going to get you.

Marion Don't.

Laurence Look at the hyaena.

Marion No. Come on. Let's go for a coffee.

Laurence We walked back along Castle Street and crossed over to go into the Cadena.

FIVE

Waiter Can I help you, sir?

Laurence Two coffees, please.

Waiter That's two coffees. Anything else?

Laurence Anything else?

Marion No thank you.

Waiter That's two coffees, then.

Laurence Yes.

Marion It's warm in here. It was beginning to get quite chilly.

Laurence What you doing tomorrow?

Marion Gonna wash my hair. You?

Laurence I dunno. Nothing. Shall I see you dinner time?

Marion Yes.

Laurence In the canteen?

Marion I'm bringing sandwiches if it's like today.

Laurence Sandwiches? No.

Marion If it's nice, yes.

Laurence Coming to the Kennard Saturday?

Marion Oh. No, I want to go to the City Hall.

Laurence Oh. Blimey.

Marion Well, it's nicer.

Laurence And it's dearer.

Marion Come on. Yeah?

Laurence All right.

Marion Here we are. Two coffees.

Laurence Thank you.

Marion All right?

Laurence Yes. Thank you.

Marion I could do with this.

Laurence Me and all.

Marion Listen, Laurence. What am I going to tell my mother?

Laurence Oh. Don't.

Marion Why won't you?

Laurence I will. I will.

Marion When though?

Laurence Oh, come on. Leave it for tonight. OK? Drink your coffee.

Marion You're selfish, you are. You are. You're selfish.

Laurence Drink your coffee.
We drank our coffee and when we had finished, I asked for the bill.

Waiter Thank you, sir.

Marion Let me pay for mine.

Laurence No. Don't be daft. What shall I leave for the tip?

Marion I don't know.

Laurence That'll have to do. Come on.
We walked out and along Castle Street to Duke Street, and across to the bus stops outside Marments.

Marion I must put my cardigan on. It's quite cold.

Laurence Yeah.

Marion And look how dark it's got. Here's your bus.

Laurence No. I'll wait with you.

Marion You don't have to.

Laurence Yes. What you doing Sunday?

Marion I don't know. Why?

Laurence I just wanted to know.

Marion Do you want to go somewhere?

Laurence No. I just wanted to know.

Marion Why you being so mysterious?

Laurence I'm not.

Marion You are.

Laurence Come on. Here's your trolley.

Marion Tell me.

Laurence Come on. Get on.

Marion Gimme a kiss then.

Laurence Come on. See you tomorrow.

Marion Goodnight.

SIX

Laurence It was quite dark when I got home. The street was empty. The sounds of the evening had gone. The children long since called in.

Woman's Voice Chilly now, Laurence.

Laurence Yes.

Woman's Voice Your father's in.

Laurence Goodnight.
I let myself in through the front door.
Aye. Aye.

Harry Is that you, son?

Laurence Yes. Jimmy not in?

Harry He won't be long now, I know him.

Laurence I went to the mirror to check if there was any lipstick on my collar. There wasn't any lipstick on my collar. Why was I checking for lipstick which I knew wasn't there? It's not as if my father would notice, or say if he did. I felt for my handkerchief in my pocket. Why was I doing this? Why was I feeling guilty about feeling guilty? Pray, father, give me your blessing and get off my back. There are other things to worry about without this worrying me. Churchill is Prime Minister. People are going to the Museum to look at the Queen's Coronation dress. My uncle is still singing the praises of Eamonn de Valera. My father listens to *Down Your Way*. The BBC is run by people who think the druids went to chapel. My girlfriend likes Dickie Valentine and I hate my job. And my mother's dead. And we can't get over it and she's not here to say, 'What's on your handkerchief? Ttt. I don't know. You be careful.' I am careful. That's all I am is careful. And I can't make retribution and I can't wear this shirt again, can I?

Harry What say?

Laurence What do you think?

Harry What, son?

Laurence Will I get away with wearing this shirt in the morning?

Harry Aye. Course you will.

Laurence No. I'd better iron a clean one.

Harry Aye. I saw David.

Laurence What was he doing over here?

Harry She was down her mother's.

Laurence He all right?

Harry He looks thin. He's working too hard. He worked a doubler. He asked if we'd heard from Christopher.

Laurence What you say?

Harry I said we'd had a card.

Laurence Yeah. A month ago. It's cold in here. Do you want me to put a match to the fire?

Harry No. I only just laid it for the morning.

Laurence We mightn't need it in the morning.

Harry No, leave it. Aye, aye. Here he is.

Jimmy Aye. Aye.

Harry You're late. Where you been till this time?

Jimmy What do you want to know where I've been?

Laurence And so it went again. But my father wasn't the skilled interrogator that my mother had been. Not that she would have got anything out of him. But the questioning would have been more thorough.

Do you want a cup of tea?

Harry I won't have one. He'll have one though.

Laurence Will you?

Jimmy What?

Laurence Will you have a cup of tea, unc?

Jimmy Aye. I don't mind, if you're making one.

Laurence I'd better do the sandwiches.

Harry I'll do mine.

Laurence What do you want?

Harry What have you got?

Laurence Cheese, cooked ham, tomatoes. The usual wide selection.

Harry I'll have ham, Laurence.

Laurence What'll you have, unc?

Harry He'll have what you give him.

Laurence I'll put the kettle on.

Harry Aye, Laurence. Put some pickle on mine.

Laurence I made their sandwiches. Ham for one, cheese for the other. And when I had finished I wrapped them in greaseproof paper and put them in paper bags and stowed them in their working jackets hanging on the back door. Then I made the tea.
Here you are.

Jimmy Thank you, Laurence.

Laurence You sure?

Harry Quite sure, son? Thank you.

Laurence What are you doing Sunday?

Harry What do you mean?

Laurence You going out Sunday afternoon?

Harry No. No. Why?

Laurence Nothing. I might ask someone over.

Harry I could go out.

Laurence No. No. I didn't mean that. I mean is it all right?

Harry What do you mean? Of course it's all right. He'll be in, mind.

Laurence That's all right.

Jimmy What's that?

Harry He's got a visitor coming Sunday.

Jimmy Oh aye.

Laurence You going to be in?

Jimmy I dunno.

Harry Of course he's going to be in.

Laurence What would she make of this shabby room? Of them? Of me and them? What would we have for tea? Would I get salad cream?

Harry Well, I'm off. You want the clock, Jimmy?

Jimmy Aye.

Harry Don't forget to wind it.

Jimmy I won't forget. Blimey.

Harry Goodnight. God bless.

Laurence Goodnight. I'd better iron my shirt.

Jimmy This time?

Laurence Aye.

Jimmy So you got a friend coming Sunday, then?

Laurence Aye.

Jimmy Do you want us to look tidy?

Laurence No. You're all right.

Jimmy Right then, I'm off. I'd better wash this.

Laurence Leave it. I'll wash it now.

Jimmy Where's the clock?

Laurence Will you call me before you get out?

Jimmy Aye. Goodnight.

Laurence Goonight.

Jimmy It was a lovely day.

Laurence Aye.

Jimmy I wonder what it will be like tomorrow?

Laurence Aye. Goodnight.

He went up to bed. I plugged the iron in. I took his cup and went into the kitchen and when I had washed it I put it away and emptied the teapot and made things ready for the morning. I went back into the living room and took a shirt from the pile of clean laundry on the window ledge and began to iron it. Yeah. It was a lovely day and it had been a lovely evening. Hadn't it?